THE SCOTCH-IRISH AMERICANS

Robin Brownstein
and
Peter Guttmacher

CHELSEA HOUSE PUBLISHERS

New York   New Haven   Philadelphia

Cover Photo: Minnie Knox, a widow who lived with her daughter in Garret County, Maryland, poses in the doorway of her log cabin in 1937.

Editor-in-Chief: Nancy Toff
Executive Editor: Remmel T. Nunn
Managing Editor: Karyn Gullen Browne
Copy Chief: Juliann Barbato
Picture Editor: Adrian G. Allen
Art Director: Giannella Garrett
Manufacturing Manager: Gerald Levine

Staff for THE SCOTCH-IRISH AMERICANS
Senior Editor: Sam Tanenhaus
Assistant Editor: Bert Yaeger
Deputy Copy Chief: Ellen Scordato
Editorial Assistant: Theodore Keyes
Picture Researcher: PAR/NYC
Designer: Noreen M. Lamb
Layout: Louise Lippin
Production Coordinator: Joseph Romano
Cover Illustrator: Paul Biniasz
Banner Design: Hrana L. Janto

Library of Congress Cataloging-in-Publication Data

Brownstein, Robin.
  Scotch-Irish Americans.

  (The Peoples of North America)
  Bibliography: p.
  Includes index.
  Summary: Discusses the history, culture, and religion of the Scots-Irish, factors
encouraging their emigration, and their acceptance as an ethnic group in North America.
    1. Scots-Irish—United States—Juvenile literature
[1. Scots-Irish—United States] I. Guttmacher, Peter.
II. Title. III. Series.
E184.S4B68   1988   973'.049163   87-26821
ISBN 0-87754-875-7

CONTENTS

THE PEOPLES OF NORTH AMERICA

CHELSEA HOUSE PUBLISHERS

A NATION OF NATIONS

Daniel Patrick Moynihan

The Constitution of the United States begins: "We the People of the United States . . ." Yet, as we know, the United States is not made up of a single group of people. It is made up of many peoples. Immigrants from Europe, Asia, Africa, and Central and South America settled in North America seeking a new life filled with opportunities unavailable in their homeland. Coming from many nations, they forged one nation and made it their own. More than 100 years ago, Walt Whitman expressed this perception of America as a melting pot: "Here is not merely a nation, but a teeming Nation of nations."

Although the ingenuity and acts of courage of these immigrants, our ancestors, shaped the North American way of life, we sometimes take their contributions for granted. This fine series, *The Peoples of North America,* examines the experiences and contributions of the immigrants and how these contributions determined the future of the United States and Canada.

Immigrants did not abandon their ethnic traditions when they reached the shores of North America. Each ethnic group had its own customs and traditions, and each brought different experiences, accomplishments, skills, values, styles of dress, and tastes in food that lingered long after its arrival. Yet this profusion of differences created a singularity, or bond, among the immigrants.

The United States and Canada are unusual in this respect. Whereas religious and ethnic differences have sparked intolerance throughout the rest of the world—from the 17th-century religious wars to the 19th-century nationalist movements in Europe to the near extermination of the Jewish people under Nazi Germany— North Americans have struggled to learn how to respect each other's differences and live in harmony.

Millions of immigrants from scores of homelands brought diversity to our continent. In a mass migration, some 12 million immigrants passed through the waiting rooms of New York's Ellis Island; thousands more came to the West Coast. At first, these immigrants were welcomed because labor was needed to meet the demands of the Industrial Age. Soon, however, the new immigrants faced the prejudice of earlier immigrants who saw them as a burden on the economy. Legislation was passed to limit immigration. The Chinese Exclusion Act of 1882 was among the first laws closing the doors to the promise of America. The Japanese were also effectively excluded by this law. In 1924, Congress set immigration quotas on a country-by-country basis.

Such prejudices might have triggered war, as they did in Europe, but North Americans chose negotiation and compromise, instead. This determination to resolve differences peacefully has been the hallmark of the peoples of North America.

The remarkable ability of Americans to live together as one people was seriously threatened by the issue of slavery. It was a symptom of growing intolerance in the world. Thousands of settlers from the British Isles had arrived in the colonies as indentured servants, agreeing to work for a specified number of years on farms or as apprentices in return for passage to America and room and board. When the first Africans arrived in the then-British colonies during the 17th century, some colonists thought that they too should be treated as indentured servants. Eventually, the question of whether the Africans should be viewed as indentured, like the English, or as slaves who could be owned for life, was considered in a Maryland court. The court's calamitous decree held that blacks were slaves bound to lifelong servitude, and so were their children.

America went through a time of moral examination and civil war before it finally freed African slaves and their descendants. The principle that all people are created equal had faced its greatest challenge and survived.

Yet the court ruling that set blacks apart from other races fanned flames of discrimination that burned long after slavery was abolished—and that still flicker today. The concept of racism had existed for centuries in countries throughout the world. For instance, when the Manchus conquered China in the 13th century, they decreed that Chinese and Manchus could not intermarry. To impress their superiority on the conquered Chinese, the Manchus ordered all Chinese men to wear their hair in a long braid called a queue.

By the 19th century, some intellectuals took up the banner of racism, citing Charles Darwin. Darwin's scientific studies hypothesized that highly evolved animals were dominant over other animals. Some advocates of this theory applied it to humans, asserting that certain races were more highly evolved than others and thus were superior.

This philosophy served as the basis for a new form of discrimination, not only against nonwhite people but also against various ethnic groups. Asians faced harsh discrimination and were depicted by popular 19th-century newspaper cartoonists as depraved, degenerate, and deficient in intelligence. When the Irish flooded American cities to escape the famine in Ireland, the cartoonists caricatured the typical "Paddy" (a common term for Irish immigrants) as an apelike creature with jutting jaw and sloping forehead.

By the 20th century, racism and ethnic prejudice had given rise to virulent theories of a Northern European master race. When Adolf Hitler came to power in Germany in 1933, he popularized the notion of Aryan supremacy. "Aryan," a term referring to the Indo-European races, was applied to so-called superior physical characteristics such as blond hair, blue eyes, and delicate facial features. Anyone with darker and heavier features was considered inferior. Buttressed by these theories, the German Nazi state from

1933 to 1945 set out to destroy European Jews, along with Poles, Russians, and other groups considered inferior. It nearly succeeded. Millions of these people were exterminated.

The tragedies brought on by ethnic and racial intolerance throughout the world demonstrate the importance of North America's efforts to create a society free of prejudice and inequality.

A relatively recent example of the New World's desire to resolve ethnic friction nonviolently is the solution the Canadians found to a conflict between two ethnic groups. A long-standing dispute as to whether Canadian culture was properly English or French resurfaced in the mid-1960s, dividing the peoples of the French-speaking Quebec Province from those of the English-speaking provinces. Relations grew tense, then bitter, then violent. The Royal Commission on Bilingualism and Biculturalism was established to study the growing crisis and to propose measures to ease the tensions. As a result of the commission's recommendations, all official documents and statements from the national government's capital at Ottawa are now issued in both French and English, and bilingual education is encouraged.

The year 1980 marked a coming of age for the United States's ethnic heritage. For the first time, the U.S. Census asked people about their ethnic background. Americans chose from more than 100 groups, including French Basque, Spanish Basque, French Canadian, Afro-American, Peruvian, Armenian, Chinese, and Japanese. The ethnic group with the largest response was English (49.6 million). More than 100 million Americans claimed ancestors from the British Isles, which includes England, Ireland, Wales, and Scotland. There were almost as many Germans (49.2 million) as English. The Irish-American population (40.2 million) was third, but the next largest ethnic group, the Afro-Americans, was a distant fourth (21 million). There was a sizable group of French ancestry (13 million), as well as of Italian (12 million). Poles, Dutch, Swedes, Norwegians, and Russians followed. These groups, and other smaller ones, represent the wondrous profusion of ethnic influences in North America.

Canada, too, has learned more about the diversity of its population. Studies conducted during the French/English conflict showed that Canadians were descended from Ukrainians, Germans, Italians, Chinese, Japanese, native Indians, and Eskimos, among others. Canada found it had no ethnic majority, although nearly half of its immigrant population had come from the British Isles. Canada, like the United States, is a land of immigrants for whom mutual tolerance is a matter of reason as well as principle.

The people of North America are the descendants of one of the greatest migrations in history. And that migration is not over. Koreans, Vietnamese, Nicaraguans, Cubans, and many others are heading for the shores of North America in large numbers. This mix of cultures shapes every aspect of our lives. To understand ourselves, we must know something about our diverse ethnic ancestry. Nothing so defines the North American nations as the motto on the Great Seal of the United States: *E Pluribus Unum*—Out of Many, One. ❧

*Soldier-statesman Sam Houston
leads the charge at San Jacinto,
Texas, against Mexican forces,
who lost the battle and control
over Texas in 1836.*

A LEGACY OF SPIRIT

On April 21, 1836, a ragtag band of soldiers collected near the San Jacinto River in southeast Texas. Defenders of the newly formed Republic of Texas, they awaited the arrival of their enemy, the Mexican army, led by President Antonio López de Santa Anna. Although outnumbered two to one, the small troop defeated Santa Anna's army at the Battle of San Jacinto and thus secured Texan independence. The leader of the small army was General Sam Houston, whose name remains synonymous with Texas. He served as the republic's first president and later, when Texas became America's 28th state in 1845, represented its interests in the U.S. Senate. In 1859 Houston was elected governor. Today the nation's sixth-largest city (according to the 1980 Census) bears his name.

Sam Houston's success completed a line of energetic pioneering that began in 1689, when Houston's great-great-grandfather made the hazardous ocean crossing from Northern Ireland to North America. His son Robert—Sam's grandfather—moved his family from Philadelphia to Virginia. When the 13 American colonies rose up to defy Great Britain in the revolutionary war, another Robert Houston—Sam's father—served as a captain under General George Washington. In 1806, Robert Houston led his family west from Virginia to the Tennessee frontier, when his son Sam was 13.

As this illustration from his almanac shows, Scotch-Irish frontiersman Davy Crockett wildly exaggerated pioneer adventures—especially his own.

The Houstons belonged to an ethnic group that played a major role in American history during its formative years. This group, known as the Scotch-Irish, immigrated to North America from Ulster, or Northern Ireland, after migrating there from Scotland. The term *Scotch-Irish* is actually an American invention, first coined in 1695. Initially, the immigrants themselves shied away from the term, preferring to describe themselves as Ulster-Scots, as they had in their homeland. Moreover, they associated the new name with "Scotch-Irish Lyllibolaro," a derogatory phrase used by the Irish Catholics in Ulster. By 1757, however, the label *Scotch-Irish* had become a fixture in the vocabulary of the colonies. The term fell into disuse for several decades after the American Revolution. In the mid-19th century it was revived by the Ulstermen themselves, who wanted to avoid being confused with a different wave of immigrants—Irish Catholics—who came to North America in the 1840s.

Theodore Roosevelt—U.S. president from 1901 to 1909—wrote: "The backwoodsmen were American by birth and parentage, and of mixed race; but the dominant strain in their blood was that of the Presbyterian Irish—the Scotch Irish, as they are often called. . . . Mingled with the descendants of many other races, they nevertheless formed the kernel of the distinctively and intensely American stock . . . fitted to be Americans from the very start."

The qualities that distinguished Scotch-Irish pioneers were embodied in the frontiersman Davy Crockett (1786–1836), who often bragged about his exploits in colorful language:

I'm that same David Crockett, fresh from the backwoods, half-horse, half-alligator, a little touched with the snapping turtle; can wade the Mississippi, leap the Ohio, ride upon a streak of lightning, and slip without a scratch down a honey locust; can whip my weight in wild cats—and if any gentleman pleases, for a ten dollar bill, he may throw in a panther—hug a bear too close for comfort, and eat any man opposed to Jackson!

During the 18th and 19th centuries, Scotch-Irish immigrants were on the move throughout the colonies, fighting Indians and spearheading frontier settlements from New England to the South.

The Scotch-Irish love for colorful storytelling, or "tall tales," enriched America's common speech. Such lively phrases as "getting mad as a meat axe" and having "an axe to grind," "sitting on the fence" instead of "going the whole hog," or becoming so intoxicated you "couldn't hit the wall with a handful of beans" are part of the linguistic legacy created by Ulster immigrants who settled in the Appalachian Mountains. Even the expression "you-all," identified with the American South, has its roots in the Scotch-Irish translation of the second-person plural form of address. One Scotch-Irish word that has long been in everyday English usage is *cabin*, the term for the log houses first designed by German immigrants and later the traditional symbol of American frontier life.

The people who lived in these cabins had a toughness that showed both in earlier and succeeding generations. In the 20th century, John Kenneth Galbraith—the economist and onetime U.S. ambassador to India—recalled the sometimes startling appear-

Supporters of the American Revolution tar and feather a British tax collector in Boston, Massachusetts.

16

ance of people of Scotch-Irish descent whom he knew during his childhood in Canada:

> [I]t was evident at a glance that they were made to last. Their faces and hands were covered not with a pink or white film but a heavy, red parchment designed to give protection in extremes of climate for a lifetime. It had the appearance of leather, and appearances were not deceptive. This excellent material was stretched over a firm bony structure on which the nose was by all odds the most prominent feature.

Scotch-Irish women were equally robust. Like the men, they worked from dawn till dusk, usually on farms. Their durability has been described by historian H. C. McCook:

> Stalwart of frame no doubt they were, with muscles hardened under the strain of toil; hale and hearty, vigorous and strong, able to wield the axe against the trunk of a forest monarch or the head of an intruding savage; to aid their husbands and fathers to plow and plant, to reap and mow, to rake and bind and gather. They could wield the scutching knife or hackling comb upon flaxen stocks and fibers, as well as the rod of rebuke upon the back of a refractory child. They could work the treadle of a little spinning wheel, or swing the circumference of the great one. They could brew and bake, make and mend, sweep and scrub, rock the cradle and rule the household.

Scotch-Irish pioneer families stood at the vanguard of westward expansion. Hammering out an existence in the wilderness spared them little time to refine their mode of living. They were not noted for meticulousness. An anonymous New Englander observed:

> In the more progressive families an iron skillet in the kitchen sink opened up a chance for parents and children to wash their hands and faces in the morning, a chance, I take it, that rarely hardened itself into a

rule for either. Ablution [washing] of the whole body even once a year, or ten years, or a lifetime, was a thing practically unknown for three generations.

These immigrants, indifferent to outside criticism, were hardy, vigorous, and determined to stay in their adopted land. At least 2 million people of Scotch-Irish origin came to the United States between the colonial era and the start of the 20th century.

Scotch-Irish immigrants made a far-reaching and significant impact on their new homeland. As a people whose Presbyterian faith once targeted them for religious persecution, they firmly understood and supported two principles that molded American political life: the democratic electoral process and the separation of church and state, which enabled all citizens to worship as they chose, free of government interference. In fact, the continuing presence of the Scotch-Irish helped introduce religious tolerance, at first in Virginia, then throughout the colonies, which further strengthened this important check against political and religious oppression.

The Scotch-Irish Americans helped shape the nation at a crucial time in its development. Their influence was felt at the highest plateaus of power. Ten U.S. presidents were of Scotch-Irish extraction, including Andrew Jackson (the statesman-general who brought rough-and-tumble frontier democracy to the White House from 1829–37) and Woodrow Wilson (1913–21).

Although emigration from Ulster to the United States is negligible today, it is estimated that 20 million people, or about 1 out of 12 Americans, can claim some Scotch-Irish lineage. Yet the group's awareness of its ancestry has steadily dimmed. In 1980 the U.S. Census reported that only 16,418 people actually traced their family origins to Northern Ireland; only slightly more than a third of them regarded Scotch-Irish as their sole ethnic background.

It is not surprising that the Scotch-Irish mixed genes with so many other ethnic groups. Their pioneering spirit brought them into contact with many people of vastly different backgrounds. Thus, the 1980 Census indicates a fairly even distribution of Scotch-Irish Americans in the country's various regions. Indeed, each of the four states with the largest Scotch-Irish population lies in a different part of the continent: Louisiana (the South), New York (the Northeast), Illinois (the Midwest), and California (the Far West).

Rural American culture, even today, owes much to the Scotch-Irish immigrants. The anonymous pioneers may not be as clearly visible as the Scotch-Irish leaders and folk heroes of American history, but American culture is rich in spoken, literary, and musical influences brought by these peoples. For many years American society has reflected the deep impression they made on religious life, work, and communities. ✎

A HOMELAND LIKE NO OTHER

Even before the Lowland Scots arrived in Northern Ireland (then known as Ulster), the region had experienced a violent history. According to legend, the bloodshed began in 400 B.C., when several ships participated in a frantic race across the North Channel. The prize to the winner of this contest would be rightful ownership of Ulster. The competitors included the Celtic chieftain O'Neill, who nervously eyed the front-runners closing in on the Irish coast. Desperate to win, O'Neill lopped off his right hand and hurled it from his boat onto the coast. This claim for Ulster later became woven into the legend "The Red Hand of Ulster."

About 800 years later, another Scot left an indelible impression on the Irish: Patrick, Ireland's patron saint. Born in Dunbarton, Scotland, then captured in a pirate raid and sold into slavery, Patrick eventually wound up in Ireland, where he herded cattle for six years before earning his release. Back home in Scotland, Patrick experienced a series of revelatory dreams and visions that urged him back to Ulster to teach Christianity—specifically, the Catholic doctrine—to its pagan population. By the middle of the 5th century Patrick had established missionary headquarters in Ulster's county of Armagh. Roman Catholicism soon emerged as a powerful force throughout Ireland.

Years later, England, too, became a Christian nation under King Ethelbert. Centuries of Danish and Norse occupation tested the religion's strength, but it endured—not only in England but in Wales, Scotland, and Ireland, countries overtaken by England as its sovereign reach extended in the 12th and 13th centuries. By 1500 all the British Isles belonged to the Roman Catholic church.

On October 31, 1517, a headstrong German monk named Martin Luther categorically denounced what he considered the abuses of the church hierarchy in Rome. Luther then established Protestantism in Europe, a movement based on his systematic disagreements with the Catholic church. By the time of Luther's death in 1546, the Protestant Reformation saw thousands of Europeans join the new movement, including England's King Henry VIII, who in 1534 made himself head of the Church of England, or the Anglican church. The Anglicans, though a product of the Reformation, claimed to be neither strictly Catholic nor Protestant.

In 1529, King Henry VIII of England clashed with the Roman Catholic church. He then founded the Church of England, which the Scotch-Irish refused to join.

An Irish chief falls in battle against English soldiers in 1581; such Celtic warlords often bested English invaders.

Another offshoot of the Reformation that soon took root in England was Puritanism, a stern sect built on the teachings of John Calvin, a church leader based in Geneva, Switzerland. The Puritans also were critical of the Roman Catholic church, derisively calling it the "Popish" faith. Another Protestant sect, the Knoxians, was a small group of Calvinists who followed the Scot John Knox. Opposed to any rigid hierarchy within Christian churches, Knox also advocated militant opposition to irreligious or immoral government leaders. He and another Scot, Thomas Cartwright, were the chief exponents of the Scottish Reformation and the architects of Presbyterianism, which became the country's dominant faith.

Presbyterianism was strict in many ways, but it also stressed freedom of religious thought. Conceived as a religion for the common people, it promoted no iron-handed and self-serving ruling establishment such as those that dominated the Anglican and Roman Catholic faiths. Instead, Presbyterians developed a system of presbyters (Greek for "elders") popularly elected by the members of the congregation. Thus, the church administration was not permitted to stray from the control of the faithful as a whole.

Presbyterians also believed that human eyes were so clouded by sin that divine revelation could be found only in the Bible, where God's word existed in written form. Because it was the duty of all Christians to study the Bible, Presbyterians stressed the need for literacy among the common citizenry. Thus, the Scots who migrated to Ulster and later to North America had an astonishingly high literacy rate.

The Seeds of Resentment Are Sown

At the same time that the Reformation introduced a new form of belief to Scotland, Ireland moved along a different course. Fierce descendants of the first Celtic lords still ruled the nation and disrupted the intentions of the English queen Mary I (1516–58), who attempted to secure plantations, or colonies, in Ireland. Though herself a Roman Catholic who had burned more than 300 Protestants at the stake, Mary loathed Ireland's Catholics. Her half sister and successor, Queen Elizabeth I (1533–1603), a Protestant, fared little better when the main force of opposition in Ulster, the O'Neill clan, allied with another clan, the O'Donnells, and defeated English invaders in a series of battles. But in 1602, the British fleet finally crushed the Irish chieftains, and Elizabeth's successor, James I, seized the Ulsterian lands of the Irish chieftains, Tyrone and Tyrconnel.

James wanted to populate conquered Celtic territory with English settlers who would support the English Crown, fend off vengeful raiders, and generate farm profits that could be sent back to England. James left the native Irish to inhabit bogs and forests and turned over the choicer lands to Protestants, both English and Scottish. The low cost attracted many settlers: four pence bought an acre; a few hundred pounds could purchase an entire borough; and 1,000 pounds secured an estate and a noble title for its owner. Those too poor to buy land rented it.

Good Settlers—Bad Neighbors

From 1608 to 1697, 200,000 poverty-stricken people departed the fertile soil of Lowland Scotland and crossed the North Channel to Northern Ireland. There they found productive farmland and took advantage of it. They bred livestock, cultivated crops, and developed a flourishing textile industry. And Ulster promised to be a haven of free worship for Presbyterians, who outnumbered English settlers six to one.

It soon became apparent, however, that the native population of Irish Catholics viewed their neighbors with hostility. To defend themselves, Ulster Scots teamed up with the English settlers. Cities became fortresses. In 1618, Scots encircled Londonderry, on Ulster's western perimeter, with a 24-feet-high, 6-feet-thick wall made of lime and stone. It was said later that when the Scots landed in Ulster, they fell on their knees and prayed to the Lord, then fell on the native Irish and *preyed* on them.

The Ulster venture might have failed dismally had the Scotch-Irish not turned their zeal and energy to a

Shown preaching in 1559, John Knox led the Protestant Reformation in Scotland by founding Presbyterianism, the faith upheld by Scotch-Irish colonists in Catholic Ulster (Northern Ireland).

This 17th-century map shows an English view of Ireland at the time the Scotch-Irish colonized Ulster for the English Crown.

host of ambitious enterprises, such as founding and operating the Bushmills Distillery, erected on the coast of the County Antrim. The Ulster Scots also took up linen weaving and cotton spinning in Londonderry and other towns, which became bustling centers of the burgeoning textile trade.

The Ulster Presbyterians considered themselves superior to their Catholic neighbors, but this opinion was not shared by the English authorities. Even King James I, who had been raised a Presbyterian, disliked his stubborn Scottish subjects. James's son and successor, Charles I, had even less sympathy for them. In 1632, he made Thomas Wentworth, earl of Strafford, Lord Deputy of Ireland. Wentworth tried to impose religious uniformity on Ulster, demanding that Presbyterians join the Church of England and pledge their loyalty to the Crown by taking the "Black Oath." This vow required them to break their own sacred National Covenant of Scotland. All those who disagreed were called "Dissenters" and were put on trial at the "Star Chamber," a tribunal established in Dublin, Ireland's capital. Wentworth's policy met with such resistance that he raised an army to force the Scots out of Ulster. Some emigrated to America; others went home to Scotland. Those who remained faced imprisonment.

Catholic Retaliation

As the English focused their attacks on the Ulster Scots, Irish Catholics seized the chance to wreak their own vengeance on the Protestants. In 1641 the Catholic clergy convened to discuss how to deal with the Ulster Presbyterians and decided that they would wage an all-out religious war against the Scotch-Irish heretics. Catholic priests declared Protestants to be devils and

A 1577 woodcut depicts Irish rebels attacking Dublin in 1534 in an effort to remove English authorities there.

deemed it a mortal sin for Catholics to protect Protestants. The campaign to destroy the Scotch-Irish received material and spiritual support from Pope Urban VIII.

On October 23, 1641, Catholic peasants undertook a four-month campaign to wipe out Ulster homesteaders. Less than two months later, the Scots sent a desperate letter to the English Parliament, asking for help:

> All I can tell you, is the miserable state we continue under, for the rebels daily increase in men and munitions in all parts, except in the province of Munster, exercising all manner of cruelties, and striving who can be the

King James I of England seized Ulster in 1602 and populated the territory with Lowland Scots, who became known as Ulster Scots—or, in the New World, Scotch-Irish.

most barbarously exquisite in tormenting the poor Protestants; cutting off their ears, fingers, and hands, boiling the hands of little children before their mothers' faces, stripping women naked, and ripping them up.

Eventually, the Catholic uprising was quelled and bloody reprisals commenced. It is impossible to ascertain the actual number of deaths caused by the revolt. Some priests claimed that as many as 200,000 Irish Catholics were killed. One observer put the total number of those who perished at roughly one-third of Ireland's 1.5 million inhabitants. The property of every Catholic landowner became subject to confiscation. All who were accused of plotting against the English crown were executed; other participants were banished.

Nineteenth-century British illustrator George Cruikshank depicted Irish Catholic insurgents killing Protestants in 1798; Catholics had first tried to wipe out the Protestant settlers in 1641.

More conflict arose as England's monarch King Charles began to bully his Scottish subjects. Many of them objected to the prayer book of the Church of England, forced on them by the Anglican leadership. In 1638, hostilities broke out. Charles also enraged English Puritans, who defeated his troops in the first English Civil Wars (1642–45 and 1648–49). The conflict culminated in the king's execution in 1649 and with the Puritan general Oliver Cromwell being named chairman of a ruling Council of State. (He was later called "Lord High Protector.") During this turmoil, Scotland tried to work free of England's grasp. Cromwell responded by marching into the country and triumphing despite the enemy's superior numbers. He defeated Scottish forces twice, in 1650 and again in 1651.

In 1660 King Charles I's son, Charles II, was restored to the English throne, but little changed for the persecuted Presbyterians. In the 1680s, Charles dispersed their congregations and even invalidated their marriages. Wedded couples were dragged before ecclesiastical courts and charged with fornication; their children were declared illegitimate. Presbyterians lost all their property to the Church of England. Once again, Ulsterians began to emigrate.

Charles II died in 1685. The next monarch, King James II, a Catholic, tried to turn Great Britain into a theocracy—a religious state—in which only Catholicism would be practiced. This policy failed, as did others, and James was deposed in 1688, when he fled to south-

Puritan soldier Oliver Cromwell became England's governing "Lord High Protector," following the English Civil Wars of the 1640s.

King Charles I of England (left) found powerful enemies in England's Puritans and Scotland's Presbyterians. Cromwell (right) had Charles beheaded and subsequently smashed an uprising in Scotland.

ern France. In 1689 he attempted to recapture the throne by assembling an army of Catholics that marched into Ulster and laid siege to the fortress city of Londonderry. James's bid failed in July 1690, when England's new king, William of Orange, defeated him at the Battle of the Boyne. Ulster was made safe for Protestantism—if not for Presbyterians.

Paper Daggers

James's downfall—known as the "Glorious Revolution"—spared Presbyterians almost certain massacre. Persecution persisted, however. In 1704, for instance, Presbyterians were barred from holding major civil and military offices. In a statement called the "Representation of the State of the Church," sent to Ireland's Lord Lieutenant, Ulster Presbyterian ministers listed their grievances, but they went unredressed.

Then a Presbyterian minister, William Holmes, returned from America with the encouraging news that the New England colonies offered refuge to Presbyterians. Indeed, Cotton Mather, one of New England's leading Puritan thinkers and ministers, referred to these potential émigrés as "oppressed brethren from the North of Ireland." As early as 1718, with the official encouragement of Samuel Shute, the governor of Mas-

King James II tried to turn Britain into an entirely Catholic nation, but Protestant forces thwarted him at the Battle of the Boyne in 1690.

sachusetts, Scotch-Irish families scraped together their savings and headed for the New World.

Meanwhile, the Church of England heaped indigities on the Ulster Scots. Presbyterian farmers paid excessive rents, then saw their profits sapped by tithes—"donations" to the church. As an Anglican official noted dryly in March 1728:

> The scarcity and dearness of provision still increases in the North. Many have eaten the oats they should have sowed their land with; . . . The humour of going to America still continues, and the scarcity of provisions certainly makes many quit us. There are now seven ships at Belfast, that are carrying off about 1000 passengers thither; and if we knew how to stop them, as most of them can neither get victuals nor work, it would be cruel to do it.

After being deposed in 1688, James II invaded Ulster, besieging the city of Londonderry in 1689.

Reasons for emigration multiplied as the 18th century wore on. Crop failures plagued Ulster in the 1720s, famine struck in 1741, farm rents soared in the 1770s, and the Ulster linen industry collapsed in 1772. Emigration continued at such a rate that the British government interceded. In 1803 the British Passenger Act severely limited the number of passengers British vessels were allowed to carry and greatly increased the minimum required supplies of food and water. These new regulations improved conditions on board but cut so deeply into the ships' profits that fares soared beyond the reach of many potential passengers. In the heyday of Scotch-Irish immigration, ships that carried Irish linen in exchange for American flaxseed, flour, and tobacco also squeezed in up to 500 people per crossing. Under the new rules, not more than 60 passengers could travel at one time on a passage from Londonderry to Philadelphia. Some ships broke the restriction by secretly stowing away passengers after clearing customs, but overall the number of emigrants dropped by 80 percent.

Emigration shrank further in 1807, when U.S. president Thomas Jefferson placed an embargo on American trade with Great Britain and France. The navies of both the former American foe and its friend and ally had sunk American shipping vessels. Making matters worse, the British began seizing ships from Ulster as they approached the American coast, forcing male passengers into British military service. Theobald Wolfe Tone, a firsthand witness of this practice, known as *impressment*, described his own near-abduction off the coast of Newfoundland, Canada, in 1795:

> We were stopped by three British frigates . . . who boarded us and, after treating us with the greatest insolence . . . pressed every one of our hands save one, and near 50 of my fellow-passengers, who were most of them flying to avoid the tyranny of a bad government at home, and who thus, most unexpectedly fell under the severest tyranny. . . . One of the lieutenants ordered

In the early 1800s the British government used propaganda, such as this cartoon, to discourage skilled workers from leaving for the New World.

me into the boat as a fit man to serve the king, and it was only the screams of my wife and sister which induced him to desist.

Jefferson's embargo did not stop the kidnappers. In fact, the same year the embargo went into effect, at least 13 ships from Ireland, bound for the United States, were waylaid by British warships, and 200 passengers were impressed into British military service. In 1809 Jefferson's embargo was lifted and American vessels resumed commercial activities. Once more Ulster Scots gained access to North America. The Irish government attempted to block provisions for ships carrying refugees, but with so little success that in 1811 as many as 5,000 Ulster Scots reached the United States.

The 1800s: The Grip Loosens

Between 1783 and 1812 about 100,000 people left Ulster for America. Many joined settlements already established on the frontiers of Pennsylvania, Virginia, and the Carolinas, but large numbers also collected in cities on the eastern seaboard, such as Philadelphia, New York, and Baltimore. Great Britain lifted the ineffective ban on emigration, which had previously applied to artisans. This action, combined with reduced fares and softened steerage regulations, encouraged poor families to leave Great Britain. An estimated half million Scotch-Irish arrived in North America between 1815 and 1845, the peak years of Ulster emigration. ✎

Pushing into the untamed frontier, settlers pass through the Cumberland Gap, escorted by American pioneer guide Daniel Boone.

On to the Frontier

I noticed particularly one family of about twelve in number. The man carried an ax and gun on his shoulder,—the wife, the rim of a spinning-wheel in one hand, and a loaf of bread in another. Several little boys and girls, each with a bundle, according to their size. Two poor horses, each heavily loaded with some poor necessaries. On the top of the baggage of one was an infant, rocked to sleep in a kind of wicker cage, lashed securely to the horse. A cow formed one of the company, and she was destined to bear her proportion of service. A bed-cord was wound around her horns, and a bag of meal on her back. The above is a specimen of the greater part of the poor and enterprising people, who leave their old habitations and connections, and go in quest of lands for themselves and children, with the hope of the enjoyment of independence in their worldly circumstances, where land is good and cheap.

—from the April 24, 1773, diary entry of Reverend David McClure, upon meeting Scotch-Irish settlers heading west through Pennsylvania

From the cold Canadian shores of Halifax, Nova Scotia, to sweltering Port Royal in South Carolina, Ulster immigrants landed on the eastern edge of the New World. Flooding into seaboard cities such as Boston, New York, and Philadelphia, the number of arrivals surpassed the expectations of the colonists who sponsored them. So large was the influx that in 1729, an Ulsterman, James Logan, who had risen to

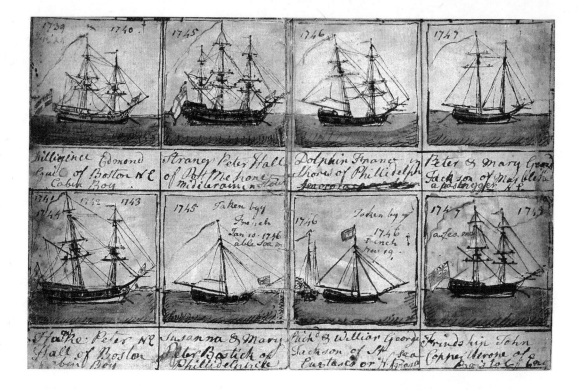

Vessels like these carried Scotch-Irish immigrants to New England during the 1740s.

the position of Pennsylvania state secretary, wrote, "It looks as if Ireland is to send all its inhabitants hither." And indeed it may have seemed that way, for in the span of the previous year, 5,605 of the 6,208 new immigrants in his state were Scotch-Irish.

Some viewed the immigrants from Ulster as rough and ready protectors. But others resented their presence. In any case, the Presbyterians, having journeyed to North America in search of freedom, continued the search after they arrived. Most immigrants from Ulster faced economic hardship and intolerance in the colonies established by earlier settlers, and many proceeded on to the desolate wilderness of the frontier. Luckily, the Ulster Scots were used to struggling.

For the vast majority of these adventuresome folk the first stop was Philadelphia, the destination of many vessels that loaded up return shipments of flaxseed there. Philadelphia, by contrast with many other towns in the Northeast, was known for its tolerance. Even there, however, immigrants discovered that English and Dutch settlers objected to their presence; so they moved on, dispersing across the eastern seaboard. After 60 years of large-scale Scotch-Irish immigration, 500 communities already existed in the United States alone: 70 in New England; 30–40 in New York; 50–60 in New Jersey; at least 130 in Pennsylvania and Delaware; more than 100 in Virginia, Maryland, and eastern Tennessee; 50 in North Carolina; and about 70 in South Carolina and Georgia.

The Northeast

New England, a refuge for so many English Puritans, offered equal promise to Scotch-Irish immigrants. Samuel Shute, the governor of Massachusetts, extended a welcoming hand to Ulsterians during the early 1700s. More good news came in 1715, when the Presbyterian minister William Holmes returned from the New England colonies with an enthusiastic account of life there. Thus, New England was the most favored destination for the first wave of Scotch-Irish immigrants. Many landed in Boston. As early as August 4, 1718, ships full of Scotch-Irish families sailed into the city's busy harbor.

Yet contrary to the encouraging words of Shute and the glowing report by Holmes, the Ulsterians were not received gladly. One reason was their poverty. "These confounded Irish will eat us all up," wrote the city's surveyor general of customs in 1719. And according to official records, from 1729 to 1742, fully two-thirds of the occupants of Boston's almshouse came from Ulster. As early as 1729 an angry mob turned away a boatload of Ulster immigrants.

Those who gained admittance into the city soon learned that Puritan communities required membership in the established church. So they moved on. Some 300 of the arrivals who disembarked in Boston in 1718 made the wilds of Maine their next destination. There, the newly arrived Scotch-Irish faced French and Indian troops and endured the paralyzing winter cold and snowfall. When spring approached, most newcomers headed inland.

They settled along the shores of the Kennebec River, and in towns christened after places in Ulster: Belfast, Bangor, Bath (originally called Cork, and sometimes Ireland), Topsham, Brooksville, Bucksport, Boothbay Harbor, Pemaquid Point, and Brunswick. Maine eventually had the largest Scotch-Irish population in New England. Many joined its growing lumber and limestone industries.

The spire of the Second Presbyterian Church towers above the streets of Philadelphia.

The existing clergy in New England assumed that the Calvinist origins of Scotch-Irish Presbyterianism would ease its followers' adjustment to Puritanism. They were mistaken. Presbyterian ministers bluntly pointed out their disagreements with Puritan beliefs. Presbyterians went as far as to avoid contact with the erring Puritans, or Congregationalists, as they were also called.

The Puritans, for their part, viewed the newcomers with increasing alarm. It was not enough that Scotch-Irish settlers willingly fended off attacks by French colonists and by Indians. They were also required to fit into the community by paying taxes that would help subsidize Puritan ministers. In Ulster, the Scotch-Irish had had their fill of tithes exacted by alien religious

Shown here is the Old State House of Boston, a city that attracted the first substantial numbers of Scotch-Irish from Ulster in the early 1700s.

An Exact Prospect of CHARLESTOWN, the Metropolis of the Province of SOUTH CAROLINA.

In 1731 South Carolina's colonial governor induced Scotch-Irish immigrants to settle in the port city of Charleston.

organizations. That the policy should resurface in New England galled them and reinforced their self-imposed isolation. Those who could afford to leave Boston moved westward to the frontier community of Worcester. But again, they ran afoul of the Puritans. At first they were mollified by the promise that in exchange for supporting the Congregationalist church they would be allowed to attend services led by their own Presbyterian ministers. But this promise proved empty and Scotch-Irish bitterness grew.

In the 1730s and 1740s, violent clashes became frequent. Puritan raiders actually destroyed Presbyterian churches under construction in Worcester. The Scotch-Irish community was incensed. About 30 families stayed on in Worcester; the rest moved on to other Massachusetts towns such as Pelham, Warren, Haverhill, Blandford, and Coleraine, or they crossed the New York border and went to Otsego.

One region where the Scotch-Irish found prosperity was New Hampshire, especially an area called Nutfield, which had an abundance of trees—chestnut, walnut, and butternut. The Scotch-Irish promptly renamed the town Londonderry. Unlike its namesake, this town needed no fortress. A Presbyterian pastor named McGregor befriended a Canadian governor named Vaudrevil, who, along with some Canadian priests, persuaded the local Indians to spare Scotch-Irish settlers from the fate met by English Puritans—scalping. In fact, the Canadians' diplomacy was so effective that the Indians shared with the Scotch-Irish their knowledge of where to fish for shad and salmon.

Londonderry rapidly flourished under Scotch-Irish stewardship. Stone houses went up; crops were planted. By 1723 a minister's residence had been built; the next year, a town meetinghouse; in six years, four schools; and by 1732 Londonderry provided one-fifteenth of the total New Hampshire tax revenues. When Scotch-Irish immigrants in this town founded the first Scotch-Irish newspaper, they contributed to the growing American interest in journalism. In fact, one of the greatest of American newspapermen was descended from Scotch-Irish residents of Londonderry—Horace Greeley. By the time of the American Revolution, at least 10 other towns were thriving in New Hampshire, thanks to the hardworking immigrants from Ulster.

Settling in New York

The first Presbyterian congregations appeared on Long Island, New York, in the 1640s. Before 1700, many had been established in New York City. Among their first and most influential ministers was Francis Make-

Early Puritan colonists hold Native American warriors at bay with their flintlocks.

The sudden influx of Scotch-Irish immigrants into America brought many paupers to almshouses like this one in Philadelphia.

mie, the "Father of American Presbyterianism," who was born around 1658 and lived until 1708, a year after he was arrested and imprisoned for preaching a religion practically regarded as heresy by its most vociferous opponents.

Religious oppression did not prevent the immigrants from pushing out along the banks of the Wallkill River, an area they dubbed Orange County in commemoration of Ulster's national color. In the first half of the 18th century the towns of Goshen and Monroe became Scotch-Irish outposts. Similarly, the western shores of the Hudson River gave rise to communities with evocative names, such as Greene, Orange, Ulster, and Sullivan counties.

In New York, religious discord was not the only hazard. On October 11, 1778—during the American Revolution—members of the Scotch-Irish settlement at Cherry Valley fled from an Indian attack that took 48 lives. Supporters of British rule in the American colonies (called *Tories*) had persuaded the Indians to join them in fighting the rebels. Many of those slain were women and children. The remaining inhabitants were taken prisoner and their community burned to the ground. Reconstruction did not get under way until seven years later.

Ulster artisans made the banks of the Hudson River a center for cotton spinning and weaving. New Jersey was well on its way to becoming a Presbyterian enclave.

Perth Amboy was one of the most conspicuous centers because of its Scottish-sounding name. By 1750 Princeton was a religious center and home of Princeton University, founded by Ulster Scots.

Pennsylvania and Through the Cumberland Gap

By 1725, most of the ships carrying Ulster immigrants bound for America had steered from Puritan New England to the more tolerant ports of William Penn's Quaker colonies. The Delaware shores, and in particular the harbor of Philadelphia, took in immigrants by the thousands. Pennsylvania became the center for Scotch-Irish settlements in the New World and the starting point for the massive immigrant flow to the south and west.

Many of these Presbyterians adjusted to Quaker society, joining the English and Germans to play a role in formulating democratic principles and establishing independence for the colonies. Those who were dissatisfied or unable to adjust pushed on to the frontier. A 1720 ordinance that excluded them from paying taxlike *quitrents* made the Scotch-Irish a unique, tolerated class of frontier protectors for the pacifist Quakers. This was, of course, music to the ears of immigrants. Unfortunately, there was a steep political price for these economic benefits. Once in the wilds of the frontier, they would be denied political representation in the colonial assembly and left militarily unprotected from Indian attack. Years later, resentment about these problems boiled over into formal protest in the 1764 march of the Paxton boys on Philadelphia.

Scotch-Irish settlers traveled westward up the Delaware River, past the Susquehanna, and through the Cumberland gap into the fertile valley of the Cumberland mountains. Along the way they far exceeded their Quaker sponsors' expectations as skillful Indian fighters. These Ulstermen were already hardened to the vio-

(*continued on page 57*)

A PRESIDENTIAL HERITAGE

Andrew Jackson (overleaf and above), nicknamed "Old Hickory," parlayed an impressive military career and his reputation as the "people's candidate" into a two-term presidency with campaign victories in 1828 and 1832; James K. Polk (below) and James Buchanan (right) supported the Jackson administration while serving in Congress; Polk later became the 11th president (1844–1848) and Buchanan the 15th (1857–1861).

51

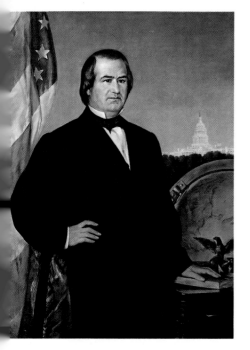

Andrew Johnson (left) took over the presidency in 1865, after Abraham Lincoln's assassination, and attempted to continue Lincoln's tolerant reconstruction program; Democratic party leaders hoped to nominate Ulysses S. Grant (right) as their presidential candidate in 1868, but a dispute with Andrew Johnson over the punishment of Confederate leaders drove Grant to the Republican camp.

Grant (leading troops above) developed a reputation for unwavering loyalty and determination as the leader of the Union Army during the Civil War; Jefferson Davis (left) faced a nearly impossible task as the first and only president of the Confederacy.

The elections of 1888 and 1892 pitted two Scotch-Irish candidates against each other—Democrat Grover Cleveland (above) and Republican candidate Benjamin Harrison (right). Harrison was elected in the first contest, but Cleveland prevailed in 1892, making him the only United States president to serve two nonconsecutive terms (1884–88 and 1892–96). Cleveland (upper right corner) rides in a carriage with the man he succeeded as president in 1888, another Scotch-Irishman, Chester A. Arthur; William McKinley (lower right corner) was assassinated in September 1901, shortly after the beginning of his second presidential term.

Woodrow Wilson, a noted historian and president of Princeton University, became the 28th U.S. president in 1912 and won reelection in 1916. A talented orator as well as a scholar, Wilson led the United States into World War I, guiding the country through the war and the Allied victory. His family traces its roots back to Ulster, where his paternal grandfather was born.

(continued from page 48)

lent repercussions of taking another's land. They regarded Native Americans as an impediment to the progress of white civilization, and the immigrants were sometimes so bloodthirsty that they threatened any hope of peaceful coexistence with the local tribes. Some outcries of protest arose in Philadelphia and other cities, but this merciless policy toward the Indians continued. The Scotch-Irish were also difficult neighbors to other immigrants in Pennsylvania. In the predominantly German counties of Lancaster and York, the two groups were so fiercely at odds that the Scotch-Irish had to be bought off to relocate to the Cumberland Valley. Once they took land for their own it was almost impossible to get them off of it. Squatting on almost any unoccupied land, they countered Quaker complaints with the simple assertion that colonists had been solicited and they, as colonists, had simply arrived as summoned. In 1743, the successor to their original benefactor, state secretary Logan, tried dispossessing these tenacious immigrants from 40,000 acres of prime land in Lancaster County. His surveyors were met with a contingent of 70 Scotch-Irish so formidable that the Quakers eventually compromised by selling them the land for a nominal sum.

A flatboat carries emigrants, with their houses and livestock, down the Tennessee River during the mid-1800s.

In this photo from the early 1900s, a Scotch-Irish farmer displays two of his horses on his homestead in Manitoba, Canada.

In 1730, temporarily deflected by the foothills of the Allegheny Mountains, the flow of Scotch-Irish migration took a southwesterly course into western Maryland, the Shenandoah Valley of Virginia, and the back country of the Carolinas. Although cities saw increasing numbers of Scotch-Irish artisans in the weaving and spinning trade, the majority of immigrants along the frontier chose farming as a means of subsistence.

The Bold March South and West

By the 1750s, Scotch-Irish settlements existed all along the Great Wagon Road that ran 700 miles beside the Appalachian Mountains from Pennsylvania to Georgia. The New World was a land of opportunity, but pioneers had to be able to think on their feet, keep their tongues from wagging, and be ready to fight for what they wanted. The Reverend John McMillan illustrated this point with an anecdote in his writings of the 1830s. On his way with the Reverend Joseph Patterson to a

Pittsburgh Presbytery meeting, both clerics stopped at a local inn for a couple of glasses of whiskey. Before imbibing, McMillan suggested a prayer and blessing. Patterson obliged with a blessing of considerable length, and as he finished, he looked down to see that both whiskey glasses before him were drained. Mc-Millan, his thirst well quenched, said, "My brother, on the frontier you must watch as well as pray."

Independent communities of North Carolinian and Virginian Scotch-Irish were in existence by 1730. These settlements were tightly knit and remained, for the most part, separate from other denominations. One such community was established at the Virginia junction of the Shenandoah and Potomac Rivers by Scotch-Irish descendant Robert Harper in 1734. The ferry he established there gave the town its name—Harper's Ferry. This locality became a crucial battleground in the Civil War more than a century later. Shortly before the war, radical antislavery leader John Brown launched one of his most defiant and violent actions there in 1859. North Carolina's Scotch-Irish population flourished under the benevolent hand of Scots governor Gabriel Johnston between 1734 and 1752. The area's exceptionally mild climate, rich soil, and peaceful Catawba Indian tribe attracted a healthy flow of immigrants from the north.

South Carolina's devastating Yamasee War with the Indians in 1715 and the rapidly growing slave population gave rise to the active soliciting of Scotch-Irish settlers in 1731. To Protestants who agreed to settle 60 miles inland from Charleston, Governor Robert Johnson offered free passage from Europe, land grants, and a 10-year quitrent exemption. Belfast immigrants soon colonized townships such as Williamsburg, which became a center for the manufacturing of the blue dye indigo.

Not all the recruited Scotch-Irish got what they expected, however. Robert Witherspoon wrote of one child's voyage to Charleston, which lasted 75 tempest-

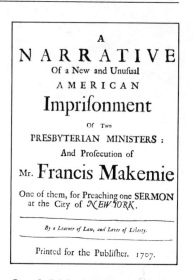

A
NARRATIVE
Of a New and Unusual
AMERICAN
Imprisonment
Of Two
PRESBYTERIAN MINISTERS:
And Prosecution of
Mr. Francis Makemie
One of them, for Preaching one SERMON
at the City of NEW YORK.

By a Learner of Law, and Lover of Liberty.

Printed for the Publisher. 1707.

Scotch-Irish churchman Francis Makemie preached before America's earliest Presbyterian congregations in colonial New York; in 1707 he went to prison for his beliefs.

tossed days, during which the child's grandmother died at sea. And the destination that met this young immigrant sounds more harrowing than welcoming.

> We landed in Charleston three weeks before Christmas. We found the inhabitants very kind. We staid [*sic*] in town until after Christmas, and were put on board an open boat, with tools and a year's provisions, and one still-mill. They allowed each hand upwards of sixteen, one axe, one broad hoe, and one narrow hoe. Our provisions were Indian corn, rice, wheaten flour, beef, pork, rum, and salt. . . . When we came to the Bluff, my mother and we children were still in expectation that we were coming to an agreeable place. But when we arrived and saw nothing but a wilderness, and instead of a fine timbered house, nothing but a mean dirt house, our spirits quite sank. . . . We were soon comforted, but evening coming on, the wolves began to howl on all sides. We then feared being devoured by wild beasts, having neither gun nor dog nor any door to our house.

In 1778, Indian warriors allied with colonists loyal to the British and massacred 48 Scotch-Irish settlers in Cherry Valley, New York.

The initial failed attempts to colonize western Georgia in the 18th century were revived by the immigrant flow down from the Carolinas, Virginia, and Pennsylvania. Georgia's frontier was more exposed to hostile attacks than the states to its north, and was thus unsuccessful in getting the English Crown's permission to recruit immigrants directly from British ports. This did not stop ambitious Indian traders and land speculators of Ulster ancestry from importing several hundred Scotch-Irish settlers. By 1774, they established the township of Queensborough on the Santee River.

The attacks in 1755 by the French on western Pennsylvania, Virginia, and Maryland colonists increased immigrant migration into the western Carolinas and Georgia. As the southward push from Pennsylvania met the westward wave from Carolina ports, the immigrant march turned further westward into the Ozark Mountains and Appalachia.

It was in the backwoods of the Carolinas, Tennessee, and Kentucky that the Scotch-Irish frontier settlers began to establish the legacy of the pioneer in American folklore. Perhaps more than any other group, the Scotch-Irish helped define this American archetype. They provided the authentic experiences behind the mythic American Indian fighter and trailblazer so vividly etched in the American imagination. Frontiersmen in the mold of Daniel Boone scraped and struggled through a wilderness where they enjoyed great freedom and independence but faced constant dangers. Severe weather conditions, wild animals, and Indians repeatedly tested their fortitude and drive. And though in persistent, and often embittered, turmoil with "tidewater" (eastern) political dominance, these mountain men and women were among the very first to lose their life in the fight for American freedom. By clearing and

Having already worked in mills and factories, Scotch-Irish immigrants filled the ranks of early American workers' societies.

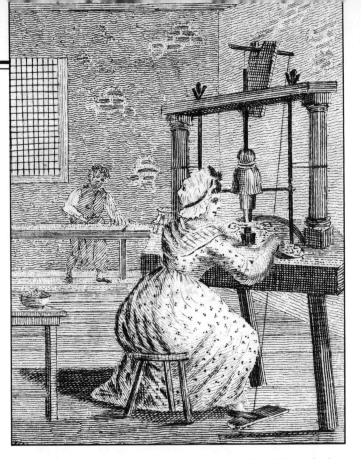

An immigrant woman operates a pin-making machine in this 1807 illustration.

cultivating the frontier, they inexorably widened the perimeter of settled territory while sowing the seeds of the pioneer spirit.

The small, rural, traditionally agricultural communities of the Appalachian Mountains are frequently referred to simply as Appalachia. The highland range is extensive—stretching as far north as Gaspé Peninsula and the St. Lawrence River valley in Canada and as far south and west as Alabama. Colonial America's intrepid Scotch-Irish pioneers built cabins and farms that are still nestled in the peaks and ravines of this rocky, mountainous region. As English, Scottish, Irish, German, and Scotch-Irish immigrants gathered here, music reverberated from firesides—sounds brought from European villages across the Atlantic. Fiddles and other instruments were taken up when the axe and plow were set aside at day's end. These European dance tunes intermingled with other styles, resulting in a uniquely

American form of musical expression. *Bluegrass* music, named for the grasses that blanket much of Appalachia, has found its way out of the backwoods and evolved into a popular American folk art. Much contemporary country and western music, because it is derived from bluegrass, also contains earlier Celtic and European influences.

Up to Canada

In about 1760 Canada became a destination for Scotch-Irish immigration. Many residents of Londonderry, New Hampshire, made their way north to establish a permanent settlement at Truro in Colchester County. Nova Scotia also rapidly became a place of settlement. At this time Alexander McNutt, another resident of the Irish city of Londonderry, arrived in Halifax with some 300 immigrants. McNutt was prepared to bring 3,000 of his compatriots to build new homes on land he owned in Nova Scotia. However, the British Board of Trade refused to allow such a large number of the Scotch-Irish to slip away from the British Isles to faraway Canada.

Large-scale immigration from Ulster to Canada did not really start until the early 19th century. By 1820 the burgeoning Canadian timber trade drew more Scotch-Irish to Canada than to the United States, though most eventually crossed the border to the United States. Ships from Ireland to Quebec and to St. John's, Newfoundland, and Halifax, Nova Scotia, offered fares as low as 30 shillings—which even at this time amounted to pocket change. Still, many passengers counted on friends and family in North America to prepay their fares. The practice became so common that in 1834 two Belfast passenger brokers noted that fully one-third of their passenger fares had been paid for in the New World. As late as the 1920s, incentives offered through the British Empire Settlement Act continued to draw Scotch-Irish immigrants to the commonwealth nation of Canada.

Iron in the Melting Pot

The Ulster immigrants did more than settle much of North America in the 18th century. They also participated enthusiastically in the continent's developing community life. This role may have come naturally to many Scotch-Irish because of Presbyterianism, which emphasized democratic procedures in church matters. Thus, its adherents had a head start in the skills that helped shape America's emerging culture.

From the moment they landed on American soil, the Scotch-Irish laid the groundwork for a Presbyterian church. They organized small local units called presbyteries guided by a single general assembly (or synod) established in Philadelphia in 1706. Almost at once the synod became the nerve center of the Pennsylvania community. Its members ruled on secular as well as religious disputes, and soon its influence spread beyond Pennsylvania's Ulster population. Before long, Dutch and English Presbyterians from New York and New Jersey found solidarity in the Philadelphia synod.

On the frontier, Presbyterianism tended to spread less rapidly. It also took on qualities that differentiated it from the church on the east coast. Not many ministers accompanied their flocks emigrating from Ulster, and fewer still headed for the frontier. Those who did served widely dispersed communities in a wilderness where dozens of miles sometimes separated the nearest neighbors. In such an environment ministers often constituted the only civil authority in existence. In addition to handling religious and moral questions, they settled property disagreements and tried to keep the peace.

In these far-flung communities, people were forced to wait for graduates from the seminaries, where ministers were trained in Latin, Greek, Hebrew, and in Biblical interpretation. There were many educational institutions that met the need for higher education and for maintaining the faith. In fact, one-fourth of the 207 permanent colleges founded in the United States before the Civil War began as Presbyterian seminaries. One of them became Princeton University.

Scotch-Irish artisans helped build colonial centers such as Boston, Philadelphia, and New York City.

Presbyterianism took root throughout North America, but it did not always flourish. The popular election of church officials, so vital to the faith, could not easily occur on the frontier, with its harsh climate, rugged terrain, and scattered population. Moreover, the synod in Philadelphia paid less attention to solving this problem than to fending off competition from other Protestant faiths. In the north, Congregationalists tried to lure Presbyterians into their chapels. In the south, the challenge came from Baptism and Methodism. ～

NAVIGATING THE MAINSTREAM

Long schooled in the democratic process of Presbyterianism, Scotch-Irish immigrants and their offspring plunged into community organizing. Such activities met with little resistance because, to other Americans, the Scotch-Irish seemed familiar and trustworthy. They spoke English, were Protestant Christians, and came from the British Isles. Unlike other Scottish immigrants, however, the Scotch-Irish had to overcome prejudices based on class distinctions. According to author Clifford Shipton, other Americans sometimes "looked down upon" the Scotch-Irish, especially in Boston. But even there, Scotch-Irish organizations sprang up as early as 1737, when the Boston Irish Charitable Society was founded—on March 17, St. Patrick's Day, the day celebrated most fervently by their long-standing enemies, the Irish Catholics. Pure coincidence led Scotch-Irish immigrants to found an organization on St. Patrick's Day. Yet on more than one occasion, these two rival groups showed unexpected amity. For instance, on St. Patrick's Day in 1771 they both collaborated to form the Friendly Sons of Saint Patrick. This organization served as a model of brotherhood between Irish Catholics and Protestants. This organization drew the majority of its members from the Scotch-Irish community, but a Roman Catholic served as its first president, and its ranks included Anglicans—

or Episcopalians, as they came to be known in the United States. The Friendly Sons assembled the Light Horse Cavalry of Philadelphia, which proved so valuable during the revolutionary war that even George Washington accepted membership in the Scotch-Irish brotherhood.

At first the social activity of Scotch-Irish Americans did not include politics. Generations of oppression at the hands of the British crown had soured the group on centralized authority, and it seemed the Scotch-Irish might grow hostile toward America once the colonies adopted the U.S. Constitution, which called for a federal system of government. The group discovered an ally in one of the country's Founding Fathers, Thomas Jefferson, who shared their fear that a strong central government might become a tyranny. Jefferson's election as the third U.S. president, in 1801, greatly eased the distrust felt by many citizens of Scotch-Irish descent. Jefferson helped prevent the Scotch-Irish from turning into hostile dissenters against the nation for whose independence they had fought.

Organized to combat Indians, the Scotch-Irish "Paxton Boys" threatened the Quaker government in Philadelphia in 1763.

Less than 30 years later, the Scotch-Irish saw one of their own elected president. Andrew Jackson, the son of Ulster immigrants, courted families on the prairies and farms and won supporters by arguing that the powers of the federal government should be sharply limited. But when Jackson's Democratic party opened its doors to the flood of Irish-Catholic immigrants, the Scotch-Irish resisted making common cause with them.

The reason for this new influx of Irish immigrants was the Great Potato Famine, which dealt Ireland a crippling blow in the 1840s. One million starved, and another 1.5 million fled. A mere 10 percent of these newcomers were Scotch-Irish, in part because previous emigration had reduced their presence in the country, and because the economic health of their heavily industrialized region, Ulster, did not depend much on farming.

As America's Irish Catholic population grew, so did Scotch-Irish animosity, although it began to surface even before the influx of Irish famine victims arrived. For example, on July 12, 1831, the streets of New York City echoed with the sound of marching and singing. "Boyne Water," "Crappies Lie Down," and other ballads commemorated the victory of William of Orange at the Battle of the Boyne 141 years earlier. These songs also taunted Catholics, some of whom had begun to take jobs away from Protestants. As the celebration wore on, scuffles broke out, then a full-scale riot erupted. In 1844 anti-Catholic rioting shook Philadelphia, destroying churches and homes. Riots based on religion broke out in New York City in 1870 and 1871.

One anti-Catholic organization followed the Scotch-Irish from Ulster to the New World: The Loyal Orange Institution, founded in Armagh County in 1795, flourished in America. By 1873 it included nearly 100 lodges in the United States and claimed 10,000 members. The institution helped keep the flame burning under the cauldron of American anti-Catholicism and eventually gave birth to many secret anti-Catholic societies, most

This page is a record of business discussed at the first presbytery—or congregation—in Philadelphia in 1706.

Built in the early 1700s at Neshaminy, Pennsylvania, the "Log College" trained young men for the Presbyterian ministry.

importantly, the American Protective Association in 1887.

The same animosity existed in Canada. James S. Graham, author of *A Scotch-Irish Canadian Yankee*, recalled schoolyard skirmishes between Protestant and Catholic boys:

> In that part of Canada the feeling between the Protestants and Catholics ran high. When the Protestant boys had a goodly number at school, we would, at noontime, get out in the yard and sing, "Up with the Orange, Down with the Green, to Hell with the Pope and God save the Queen." Then there generally was a fight but never very serious for some of my best friends were among those Catholics.

High Spirits

Anti-Catholicism was perhaps a reflex on the part of the Scotch-Irish in North America. Another cultural reflex may very well have been their abiding taste for strong drink. According to an old Appalachian saying, when English settlers arrived they built a house, the Germans built a barn, and the Scotch-Irish built a distillery. The

Ulster tradition of homemade whiskey thrived in America, where the liquor was called "white lightning," "moonshine," or "sourmash." Some of the ingredients changed, however. Corn, introduced to white settlers by the Indians, replaced the malt and grains used in the old country.

Whiskey figured prominently in the lives of Scotch-Irish frontier people. At weddings some guests consumed large quantities of spirits. Liquor flowed no less liberally at funerals, which could turn into raucous, hilarious affairs. More importantly, whiskey provided a reliable source of income in times when farming proved a struggle. Moonshine even doubled as currency with which to pay for sugar, calico, gunpowder, and other necessities.

In Ulster, the government regularly tried to tax profits made from homemade stills and sent agents to hound whiskey manufacturers. These "revenuers" or "gaugers" met with open resistance. In the words of one commentator, Horace Kephart, "The very name [gauger] invariably aroused the worst passions. To kill a gauger was considered anything but a crime[;] wherever it could be done with comparative safety, he was hunted to death."

In America the identical conflict arose in 1791, when Alexander Hamilton—of Scots descent and the United States's first secretary of the treasury—imposed an excise tax on whiskey. Outraged distillers in Pennsylvania rioted in 1794, and President Washington sent in government troops to quickly quell what became known as the Whiskey Rebellion. A later secretary of the treasury, Albert Gallatin, who served under President Jefferson, sympathized with the Scotch-Irish distillers. Gallatin had actually lived on the frontier in the 1780s and understood that homemade whiskey should be treated as a legitimate commodity. "We are distillers," he wrote, "through necessity, not choice, that may comprehend the greatest value in the smallest size and weight." Even today, backwoods distillers are known

Scotch-Irish immigrant William Tennent (1673–1746) founded the "Log College"; his followers organized the College of New Jersey.

to greet gaugers or "revenue dogs" with a blast from their shotguns.

Moonshiners had to keep more than just federal agents away from their stills. The indispensable farmyard hog, said to have a special fondness for the mash, sometimes met its death by swooning into a vat of the stuff. In fact, when a moonshiner's batch of whiskey was too strong, it was sometimes said that it "musta had a dead hog in it."

Meat, Potatoes, and Corn

Another foodstuff played an even more vital part in Scotch-Irish life than sourmash whiskey: the Irish tuber, or potato, which was introduced in Europe by Spanish explorers returning from South America. Potatoes became immensely popular in Ireland, and until the crop failure of the mid-1840s, they provided sustenance to most of Ireland's population. Immigrants

American artist George Caleb Bingham (1811–1879) painted Stump Speaking, *a depiction of politics on the frontier.*

brought potatoes to North America, mystifying many of the other colonists. According to A. L. Perry, colonists in Worcester, Massachusetts, in 1719 did not know what to do with the potatoes their neighbors gave them:

> The tradition is still lively in Scotch-Irish families . . . that some of their English neighbors, after enjoying the hospitality of one of the Irish families, were presented each, on their departure, with a few tubers for planting, and the recipients, unwilling to give offense by refusing, accepted the gift; but suspecting the poisonous quality, . . . *chucked* them into the water. The same spring a few potatoes were given for seed to a Mr. Walker, of Andover, Mass., by an Irish family who had wintered with him, previous to their departure for Londonderry to the northward. The potatoes were accordingly planted, came up and flourished well, blossomed and produced *balls* [stalk tops]. . . . They cooked the balls in various ways, but could not make them palatable, and pronounced them unfit for food. The next spring, . . . the plow passed through where the potatoes had grown, and turned out some of a great size, by which means they discovered their mistake.

Backwoods "moonshiners" produce whiskey in makeshift stills—a tradition brought to America by Scotch-Irish immigrants.

Just as the Scotch-Irish brought potatoes to North America, so they acquired a new staple there, corn, the main crop cultivated by Native Americans, or Indians, who thus helped feed the very settlers who were encroaching on their lands. Corn replaced oats and barley in the whiskey distilled by Scotch-Irish immigrants, replaced wheat flour as the main ingredient in hasty pudding, and was made into breads such as johnnycake and corn pone. These dishes supplemented a diet of mush, which consisted of ground corn and milk, often mixed with molasses, bear's oil, and fried meat gravy.

American Indians enriched the Scotch-Irish diet in many ways. The frontier had abundant wild game, which the Indians hunted expertly. Though used to farming rather than hunting, the Ulstermen soon learned how to track and kill game. Venison, rabbit, squirrel, bear, turkey, and other forest fowl appeared more commonly on Scotch-Irish dinner tables than did beef, mutton, and pork. When choice game became scarce, raccoons and opossums sufficed. Mountain streams were thick with pike, bass, catfish, suckers, chub, sunfish, trout, and eels. Dinner often concluded with fruit, when it was in season, especially apples, which made a very American pie. Another dessert was doughnuts, made with wild honey, maple sugar, or maple-molasses.

To Clothe Themselves

For the frontiersman of the 18th and 19th centuries, game animals were a source not only of food but of durable clothing. Deerskin supplied material for shirts, trousers, coats, and moccasins—shoes derived from designs originated by the Indians. Frontiersmen wore deerskin hunting shirts—loose, frocklike garments that reached halfway down the thighs and had large sleeves. The breast of the shirt served as a kind of wallet that held everything from a hunk of bread to a rag for cleaning rifle barrels. The standard hunting outfit also included deerskin—or cloth—leggings. Eventually red

Shooting for the Beef, *by George Caleb Bingham, illustrates the importance of hunting and marksmanship to frontiersmen.*

woolen jackets replaced the deerskin shirt. Another accessory, the raccoon-skin cap worn by American mountain men, sometimes doubled as currency. Nor was a belt merely for keeping one's pants up. Usually fastened from behind, it often held paraphernalia such as mittens, hatchets, hunting knives, bullet sacks, and powder horns. A heavy cape, frequently decorated with a fringe of different colors, topped off the costume.

Pioneer women wore garb that was slightly less coarse and rudimentary. Short gowns and petticoats served all year round—wool in winter and linsey-woolsey (a blend of linen and wool) in summer. The standard color, a neutral gray, could be dyed. Popular colors were red and green. Calico later became fashionable for common dress, but this fabric tended to cost a lot. Some fortunate women had silk dresses they wore

Pioneering Scotch-Irish immigrants excelled at Indian-fighting.

on special occasions, though almost none had jewelry. Most covered their feet with moccasins in the cold months and went barefoot during mild times of the year.

Hairstyles also changed. The Indian fashion of long hair had a distinct practical value: warmth. Many settlers, who had worn their hair close cropped, let their hair grow long and then coated it with bear grease for added insulation. It was then held in place with an eel skin, or *whang*. Women's headgear consisted of wool hats or hoods in winter, sunbonnets or a colored handkerchief in summer. Men had one warming feature that Indians lacked—beards, which glistened black from beneath what showed of their faces.

A Sense of Space

Clearing and cultivating land occupied many Scotch-Irish settlers in Canada and the United States. Few prospered at this activity, however. Perhaps they were ill suited to farming after so many years spent on the move—first from Scotland to Ulster, and then to America. In any case, Scotch-Irish farmers seemed to be unfamiliar with certain agricultural methods. For example, many often set up homesteads on hillsides, where the soil contained too much slate. German-American farmers, by contrast, chose fertile valleys lined with rich deposits of limestone.

Worse, Scotch-Irish frontier people misused the land, either because they did not know enough to rotate crops—which helps replenish minerals in the soil—or did not care to do it. Instead, after a plot of land was depleted of nutrients, the farmers simply moved on to the next. Many were too careless to work out even an efficient system for planting. German immigrants cleared their fields of tree stumps, whereas Scotch-Irish farmers often did nothing about removing them, with the result that the area, filled with stumps, became difficult to plow. Writer James S. Graham once described

An 1837 issue of Davy Crockett's Almanack *included sensational accounts of frontier exploits.*

A revolutionary volunteer (or Minuteman) prepares to fight the British during the American Revolution—a cause most Scotch-Irish supported.

his grandfather's unfortunate experience in Ontario, Canada, after leaving Armagh during the mid-19th century:

> Although no axman, he set about clearing fifty acres of this valuable timberland for farming purposes. After the timber was destroyed, he found the soil had little value. Had he been more experienced, he might have chosen fifty acres of hardwood land which would have been easily cleared and would have produced a rich, fertile soil for, in a few years after clearing, this land would have been free of stumps, because the hardwood stump decays rapidly while the pine stump, full of turpentine, decays very slowly and must be pulled with a stump machine at great expenses. This land would not have had the boulders and stones which were always found in pine territory. Then, too, had this pine timber been left standing, it might have brought fabulous wealth to the Graham family while the hardwood land when cleared would have given them rich acres, easily tilled.

Bare Fists and Belly Laughs

Another physical activity that the Scotch-Irish learned the hard way was fighting. Because they inhabited land that had belonged to the Indians, they often did battle with them and thus became adept at the arts of concealment and ambush. Such skills, learned from necessity on the frontier, proved invaluable when they fought a much more orderly and predictable enemy, the British redcoats, during the American Revolution.

Another kind of fighting, fisticuffs, also proved useful on the frontier, often as an effective means of letting off steam stored up under the stresses of backwoods conditions. Most accounts of their sporting fondness for roughhousing portray contests as ferocious. Rules of fair play did not usually enter into these confrontations. Writer Arthur Moore noted an English traveler's observations of Kentuckians' fondness for fisticuffs at the beginning of the 19th century:

> They fight for the most trifling provocations, or even sometimes without any, but merely to try each other's prowess, which they are fond of vaunting. . . . Their hands, teeth, knees, head and feet are their weapons, not only baring with their fists . . . but also tearing, kicking, scratching, biting, gouging each others eyes out by dexterous use of a thumb and finger, and doing their utmost to kill each other.

Equally volatile was the Scotch-Irish sense of humor. Ulster Scots had a great love for practical jokes,

A woodcut shows how Scotch-Irish and other pioneers felled trees and built log cabins on the edge of the wilderness.

especially the *charivari*, a madcap serenade given by pranksters to a bride and groom on their wedding night. The Scotch-Irish also enjoyed quick-witted sarcasm and the joke made at another's expense. As scholar A. L. Perry once explained:

> It was a pleasing and remarkable trait of these people, that they knew how to put things in a humorous and witty and even sarcastic dress. . . . Of course their brogue was a great help to them here, because it intensified the sense of incongruity, which seems to be of the essence of merriment. Subjectively they relished the sense of the grotesque and incongruous.

Ministers became particularly adroit at verbal duels. According to one anecdote, two Scotch-Irish clergymen were walking along together on an icy road. One of them slipped and fell flat. The Reverend Upright eyed his brother for a moment solemnly, and quoted: " 'The wicked stand in slippery places.' " Instantly, the Reverend Prostrate retorted, "I see they do, but I can't."

Cabin Fever

Perhaps the most symbolic, as well as practical, contributions Scotch-Irish immigrants made to American culture was popularizing the log cabin. Scandinavian settlers, who often came from heavily forested regions, built the first such houses. But practical-minded Ulster immigrants erected great numbers of them as well. As late as 1939, some 270,000 of these pioneer dwellings still were in use across the United States. Log cabins usually consisted of hewn hardwood logs stacked atop each other, their gaps plugged with mud, stone, and wood slivers, then sealed with lime mortar. Primitive and drafty, they measured about 16 by 22 feet, yet often had to accommodate families of eight or more. One inhabitant of such an abode, the Reverend John McMillan of western Pennsylvania, described his cabin in a letter written in 1832:

When I came to this country, the cabin in which I was to live was raised, but there was no roof to it, nor any chimney, nor floor. The people, however, were very kind: they assisted me in preparing my house, and on the 16th of December, I removed into it. But we had neither bedstead, nor tables, nor stool, nor chair, nor bucket. All these things we had to leave behind us, as there was no wagon road at that time over the mountains. . . . We placed two boxes, one on the other, which served us for a table, and two kegs served us for seats; and having committed ourselves to God, in family worship, we spread a bed on the floor, and slept soundly till morning.

Life on the frontier involved constant hardship, and the survival of the pioneers spelled the nation's success at extending the boundaries of its civilization into the wilderness. The forces that moved millions across the Atlantic and cast them throughout a wild new country also formed some of the most versatile and determined people on the North American continent. ∾

The Continental Congress,
which endorsed American
independence from Great
Britain, included 14
Scotch-Irishmen.

RESTLESSNESS AND ACHIEVEMENT

The descendants of Ulster did not need to be persuaded to join their fellow colonists in the struggle for independence from Great Britain. Indeed, as far back as 1627, the Puritans of the Massachusetts Bay Company had expressed a desire for self-governance with the Cambridge Agreement. This was drafted in 1628, a year after John Endecott (c. 1558–1665) sailed his ship, the *Abigail*, to what now is the city of Boston. Under the terms of the agreement, more immigrants would follow Endecott's handful of settlers as long as the company handed over governmental authority to this next wave of immigrants. What ensued was the election of John Winthrop as Massachusetts governor.

More tellingly, the 56 signers of the Declaration of Independence included 14 Scotch-Irishmen, including Thomas McKean, president of the Congress, George Taylor, James Smith, Matthew Thornton, Edward Rutledge, George Read, and William Whipple. Another Scotch-Irishman, John Witherspoon, helped ratify the Declaration of Independence. A Presbyterian minister, he was the only clergyman to serve as a representative in the First Continental Congress (the revolution's governing body from 1776 to 1779). And it was a Scotch-Irishman—Thomas McKean, in fact—whom George

Scotch-Irishman Sir Guy Carleton, called the "savior of Canada," defeated American revolutionary forces in Quebec, Canada.

Washington dispatched as his courier bearing the triumphant news of England's surrender to the Continental army at the Battle of Yorktown in October 1781.

At the outset of the conflict, the American forces crossed the border into Canada, which remained loyal to Great Britain. The leader of the American expedition, Richard Montgomery, came from Conroy, Ireland. In 1778, he died in battle at the Plains of Abraham in Quebec, after his troops were vanquished by another Scotch-Irishman, Sir Guy Carleton, Baron Dorchester—the "Saviour of Canada" and the chief commander of its armed forces. Carleton saw to it that his opponent Montgomery received a hero's burial with military honors. Carleton eventually was appointed governor of Quebec province by the British crown.

Some 80 years later, when the United States was divided by the Civil War, two generals of Scotch-Irish ancestry again found themselves on opposite sides of the conflict. In the First Battle of Bull Run, fought near Washington, D.C., in 1861, Thomas Jonathan Jackson proved that he was one of the Confederacy's most extraordinary military commanders. In this confrontation, cagier Confederate forces routed Northern troops. Because of his unflinching valor that day, he was thereafter called "Stonewall" Jackson. He again defeated the North at Cedar Mountain, where he bested General George B. McClellan, a Scotch-Irishman who commanded the entire Union army until a series of defeats led President Abraham Lincoln to relieve him of his post in 1862. His eventual replacement, the Scotch-Irishman Ulysses S. Grant, led the Union to victory and became the most honored U.S. military leader of his time.

Grant's battle plans were not noted for their elegance. Nevertheless, his bulldog tenacity and his lavish—sometimes reckless—use of manpower gradually brought the Confederates to final defeat. As a soldier, he is said to have introduced methods that later characterized modern warfare: massed troop formations and battles of attrition (gradual wearing down of the enemy). An obscure ne'er-do-well from Ohio, he rose to heroic heights in the eyes of many Northerners. Three years after the Civil War's conclusion, he was voted the Republican presidential candidate. He won election to the highest office easily, and though he gave a lackluster performance as president, he was widely admired by the public.

Two years after McClellan lost his military post, he won the Democratic nomination for president, only to lose the election to Lincoln. Other Ulstermen had better luck in their pursuit of the nation's highest office: James K. Polk, president during the Mexican War of

South Carolina's Edward Rutledge, who signed the Declaration of Independence, was of Scotch-Irish descent.

Thomas Jonathan "Stonewall" Jackson, the future Confederate general, served in the Mexican War as a lieutenant.

1846–48; the Presbyterian James Buchanan (1857–61), whose name originally had been Buch-Annan, meaning "low grounds near water"; Andrew Jackson (1829–37); Andrew Johnson (1865–69); Ulysses S. Grant (1869–77); Chester A. Arthur (1881–85); Grover Cleveland (1885–89 and 1893–97); William Henry Harrison (1841); Benjamin Harrison (1889–93); William McKinley (1897–1901), whose name translates as "son of Finlay"; and Woodrow Wilson (1913–21), who at one time taught law and economics at Princeton University and served as its president.

Of all the men on this list, none played a more central role in American history than Andrew Jackson. His parents, who had been active in the linen trade, arrived in America from the Ulster coastal town of Carrickfergus in 1765. Two years later Andrew was born in the Waxhaw Settlement on the border separating North and South Carolina. Orphaned at 14, he joined the revolutionary army and was captured by British troops in 1781. After his release, he attended law school, then moved west to Nashville, Tennessee, where he prospered as an attorney. He served as a delegate to the convention that drafted the state's constitution in 1796. Then, within a six-year period, Jackson served in the U.S. House of Representatives and the Senate, was a judge for the Tennessee superior court, and commanded the Tennessee militia.

The War of 1812 made Jackson a national figure. He achieved spectacular military success against the British at New Orleans, Louisiana, in January 1815. Nine years later, he ran for president but lost to John Quincy Adams. Still, he won many followers by advocating states' rights, which called for the federal government to give freer rein to individual states. In 1829, Jackson again ran for president and swept to victory.

Enormous crowds gathered in Washington, D.C., to see Jackson sworn in as president. Tall and lean, with a lantern-jawed face and a high forehead crowned thickly with white hair, Jackson seemed the model fron-

tiersman, a symbol of the American West. Yet his manner was dignified and courteous, covered with a genteel southern gloss. A complex man, he developed a complex—even contradictory—vision of government. His championing of the common people over East Coast big-business interests led to the Populist movement and the ideal named for him: "Jacksonian Democracy." Despite his support for frontier farmers against "money power," as he called it, he himself had grown rich practicing law.

In 1828 a controversy concerning customs duties broke out among the states. South Carolina statesman John Calhoun (also Scotch-Irish) took the position that the states could refuse to comply with congressional legislation and still retain all rights granted them by the U.S. Constitution. Thus, with Calhoun, came about the *nullifers* movement. Any law passed by Congress not to

When Andrew Jackson became the seventh president of the United States, farmers and country-dwellers converged on the capital to celebrate.

the states' liking, they claimed, could simply be nullified by the states. Jackson faced down this attack on the Union by showing that he was squarely behind using military power if necessary to enforce the laws of Congress.

Jackson acted more predictably on another issue. It involved the Bank of the United States, then the country's central financial institution. Expertly run, it earned profits for the government and for the industrialists and manufacturers whom it served. Citizens in the South and Southwest, however, were wary of the bank. Many were convinced that the institution existed solely to promote business interests in the Northeast. Jackson agreed, and his decision to veto a congressional bill meant to recharter the bank became the focus of his campaign for reelection in 1832. Jackson won handily, defeating Kentucky statesmen Henry Clay.

President Jackson forcibly expelled Native Americans from the eastern states to territories west of the Mississippi River. Their journey is known as the "Trail of Tears."

Earlier in his career, Jackson had acquired a reputation as a merciless Indian fighter by destroying the formidable Creek Indian nation. In 1830, as president, he sought to remove the Native Americans from the eastern United States to territory west of the Mississippi River, thereby expanding U.S. territory. With the army

at their backs, men, women, and children were forced to leave their ancestral homes on a journey by foot that came to be called "The Trail of Tears." Future generations came to regard this policy as misguided; it led, after all, to one of the darkest chapters in the nation's history—the systematic destruction of the country's true native population. This failure aside, Jackson did much to strengthen the office of president, and his views ultimately did much to shape the emerging Democratic party. After his death in 1845, he became the first U.S. citizen to have a Congressional statue erected in his memory.

Folk Heroes

The frontier that posed so many obstacles to Scotch-Irish pioneers also provided many opportunities for heroic men of action. One such figure was the Canadian statesman Robert Baldwin (1804–1858), who led the Upper Canadian Reformers movement that attempted to gain political freedom for Canada. Baldwin made enormous strides toward securing the establishment of the Dominion of Canada, not unlike the efforts made by Sam Houston for his beloved Texas. Another folk hero was Mike Fink, a flatboatman whose physical strength, superb marksmanship, and adventures on the Ohio River made him a mainstay of American folk tales. His occasional companion Davy Crockett referred to Fink as "a helliferocious fellow," and was a sometime partner in Fink's story.

Crockett himself was the best known of all Scotch-Irish frontiersmen and also the most boastful. A hypnotic storyteller, he often spun outlandish, self-promoting yarns, although his genuine achievements needed no exaggeration. Crockett was born in Tennessee in 1786, the son of a Scotch-Irish soldier in the revolutionary Continental army. Footloose in his youth, Davy Crockett eventually married Polly Findlay, and the pair moved to Lincoln County, Tennessee, near the

Of Scotch-Irish descent, Robert Baldwin was a Canadian political leader who worked for governmental reform and greater cooperation between Canada and Great Britain.

Although he sometimes teamed up with Davy Crockett, Scotch-Irish flatboatman Mike Fink was a frontier legend in his own right.

Alabama border. There Crockett failed as a farmer, but his gifts as a hunter and marksman soon landed him a job as a scout for General Andrew Jackson during the Creek Indian War of 1814. When the war ended, Crockett's supreme self-assurance, courage, and flair landed him a succession of jobs, first as a justice of the peace, then as a colonel in the militia, and in 1821 as a representative in the Tennessee legislature.

Soured by his first glimpse of politics, Crockett repaired to the Tennessee backwoods and resumed his favorite pastime, hunting. (Later he claimed to have killed 105 bears in a 9-month period.) But backwoods supporters coaxed him back into the political arena. In 1823 he won reelection to the Tennessee legislature. Four years later, someone jokingly suggested that Crockett run for Congress. He did and served three terms. In Washington, Crockett caused a stir as an extemporaneous speaker, who commented shrewdly, vividly, and humorously on national issues. Heedless of parliamentary constraints, Crockett began one of his speeches on the congressional floor with words to this effect:

Mr. Speaker. Who—Who—whoop—Bow—Wow—Wow—Yough. I say, Mr. Speaker; I've had a speech in soak this six months, and it has swelled me like a drowned horse; if I don't deliver it I shall burst and smash the windows.

Disagreements with President Jackson led to Crockett's defeat in 1835. He then joined the independence movement building in Texas, which sought to gain its freedom from Mexico. In March 1836 Crockett perished at the Alamo, alongside other fighters massacred by the much larger Mexican army.

Mental Explorers

Pioneer existence in America often seemed to bear out the familiar saying that necessity is the mother of invention. The arduous task of harvesting crops led Cyrus McCormick (1809–1884) to develop the mechanical reaper. The engineering genius of Robert Fulton (1765–1815) produced the steam engine that powered the majestic boats that once voyaged up and down the Mississippi River. Fulton also patented machines for sawing marble, spinning flax, and twisting hemp into rope; he invented a dredge for cutting canals and even pioneered the submarine. Another Scotch-Irish American, Samuel Morse—a painter turned inventor—perfected the telegraph in 1836. This device bridged the distance between remote outposts of the American West.

No inventor influenced people's everyday lives more than Thomas Alva Edison. He was born in Milan, Ohio, in 1847, to a mother of Scotch-Irish extraction. As a student in the classroom, Edison performed so poorly, especially in mathematics, that his teachers labeled him "addled." His mother withdrew him from school and saw to his education at home. By age 10, Edison had built himself an impressive chemistry lab, which was both feared and admired by his neighbors.

Edison's awkwardness with numbers did not stymie his entrepreneurial talent, or his great energy. In his teens he ran a railroad concession business that earned him handsome profits and gave him time and money enough to install a laboratory for the experiments in an empty baggage car. Edison's later success as an inventor stemmed from his unique combination of abilities. He

Davy Crockett's Almanack (*with Crockett on the cover*) *told of "wild sports in the west."*

had a flair for organization, a phenomenal capacity for work, and a keen commercial sense. Just as Davy Crockett scoffed at legal knowledge, Edison shunned formal scientific training and theory. Instead, he relied on his own uncanny scientific instincts.

In 1869 Edison patented his first invention, the electrographic vote recorder. He formed a consulting partnership with two other electrical engineers, then acquired enough capital to open his own full-scale laboratory. Soon he moved to Menlo Park, New Jersey, where he operated the largest private laboratory in the world. In the 1870s Edison perfected many important inventions, including the carbon telephone transmitter and the phonograph, whose patent he sold to France for $1 million, a staggering fee at the time.

Edison's greatest triumph came in 1879, when he developed the first practical light bulb and supple-

Scotch-Irish immigrants won scant praise for their farming methods, but Cyrus McCormick's invention of the reaper revolutionized farm technology.

In addition to the steam engine, Scotch-Irishman Robert Fulton invented several industrial machines and anticipated the modern submarine.

mented the breakthrough by designing an elaborate electrical system for generating light and power. In 1883 he discovered the "Edison effect," which became the basis for the radio. His 1891 "Kinetoscope," was a forerunner of motion pictures. Later he showed how moving images could be synchronized with sound. Subsequent inventions included such diverse projects as the dictating machine, the mimeograph, torpedoes, flame throwers, storage batteries, and submarine periscopes.

Edison's patents made him rich and he shrewdly consolidated his enterprises into a single company, the Edison General Electric Company. But he funneled most of his profits back into the lab, and he shunned the limelight, denying his almost mythical reputation with the oft-quoted remark, "Genius is two percent inspiration and ninety-eight percent perspiration."

Samuel Morse is recognized for his communications breakthrough— the invention of the telegraph—not for his earlier work as a painter.

As tireless as his Scotch-Irish forebears, Edison functioned well on very little sleep. He had a brusque manner, but, like his ancestors, he loved pranks. In 1920 he was awarded the Distinguished Service Medal and was elected to the National Academy of Sciences in 1927. Edison died in 1931 in Orange, New Jersey.

The Gift for Language

Presbyterians frequently had an intense passion for words—not only those written in the Bible but also those spoken in sermons and exchanged in the heat of political debate. Out of this passion grew a flourishing literature. As early as 1771 John Dunlap founded the *Pennsylvania Packet*, a literary journal that became

America's first daily newspaper. Dunlap also had the honor of being chosen to set into type both the Declaration of Independence and the Constitution of the United States.

Educator William McGuffey (1800–73) devised the first widely distributed readers—the *Eclectic Readers*—for elementary schoolchildren. These primers, which contained impressive selections from a wide variety of sources, sold more than 120 million copies during the 19th century and enlightened countless Americans. Andrew McNally founded the esteemed publishing house of Rand McNally, whose maps and atlases remain fixtures in millions of schools and households.

One of the titans of American journalism was Horace Greeley, who transformed newspapers from dull society sheets and sensationalistic rags to forums for investigative journalism and public opinion. Born in Amherst, New Hampshire, in 1811, Greeley inherited his Scotch-Irish mother's deep respect for literature—including the plays of William Shakespeare and the poems of the 19th-century Englishman George Gordon,

Thomas Alva Edison, who had Scotch-Irish ancestors on his mother's side of the family, invented so many useful devices he was called the Wizard of Menlo Park.

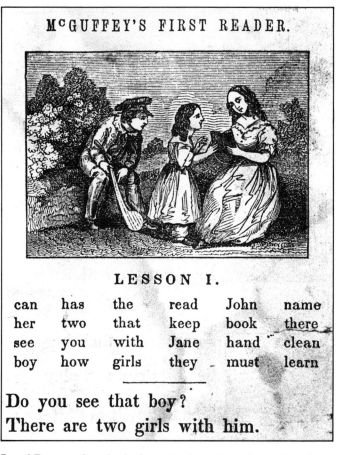

McGUFFEY'S FIRST READER.

LESSON I.

can	has	the	read	John	name
her	two	that	keep	book	there
see	you	with	Jane	hand	clean
boy	how	girls	they	must	learn

Do you see that boy?
There are two girls with him.

Lord Byron. Greeley's formal education abruptly halted when he began an apprenticeship to Amos Bliss, the editor of the *Northern Spectator*, published in East Poultney, Vermont. After the *Spectator* folded, Greeley held a series of printing jobs that eventually brought him to New York City in 1831 with about $25 in his pocket.

In New York, Greeley's provincial manner and dress made him the butt of jokes and even lost him a job at the *Evening Post*. He eked out a living as a printer and typesetter before forming a partnership with a fellow printer, with whom he worked on several publications. But Greeley wanted to be a writer, and soon he was printing articles of his own in a new paper. In

1834 he cofounded the *New Yorker*, a weekly literary and news journal. Vigorously nonpartisan, it gained many subscribers but earned little profit and eventually failed. Greeley continued to write articles for many newspapers, including the *Jeffersonian*. This publication, affiliated with the Whig party, opposed the presidency of Andrew Jackson. Greeley soon became editor of the *Jeffersonian* and branched out as a political reporter and commentator. In 1840, another publication headed by Greeley rolled off the presses: the *Log Cabin*. It met with success and led Greeley to publish the *Tribune*.

By 1846 the *Tribune* had become New York's leading newspaper. It was fearless, fair, intellectually challenging, and set a precedent for journalistic excellence. It included no gossip or society chat, printing only "hard" news, editorials, and book reviews. In the pages of the *Tribune* Greeley gave free rein to his own views: He opposed monopolies, slavery, capital punishment, and the selling of liquor; he favored labor unions and high tariffs on imported goods.

The modern newspaper format owed much to Greeley's innovations. A man of powerful convictions, he advanced causes in defense of human equality, such as the antislavery Free Soil movement. In addition, articles appeared in the *Tribune* by the European political thinker Karl Marx (father of modern socialism) and the utopian philosopher Charles Fourier. Occasionally, Greeley's opinions seemed extreme to his contemporaries, but they continued to read and applaud the *Tribune*. Greeley's simplest assertions, such as "Go West, young man, go West," had a homespun wisdom that earned their creator a place among the brightest literary lights of his day.

As Greeley's influence grew, he gravitated to politics. He served in Congress for a few months—December 1848–March 1849—and in 1856 helped found the Republican party. In 1872 Greeley captured the presidential nomination of an even newer party, the Liberal Republican, but lost by a landslide to U. S. Grant,

Horace Greeley, a Scotch-Irish New Englander, was an innovative writer, publisher, editor, and presidential aspirant.

describing himself as "the worst beaten man who ever ran for office." Crushed by this defeat, Greeley tried to recover the editorship of the *Tribune* and failed again. Both his mind and body collapsed, and in 1872 this giant of American journalism went insane and died. Bronze statues of the journalist were erected in New York City's Greeley Square, in the *Tribune* building, and at the Greenwood cemetery. Each statue commemorates a publisher, writer, and editor who expanded the horizons of journalism by courageously using freedom of the press to communicate the truth as he honestly understood it.

Captain of Finance

Although most Scotch-Irish immigrants scraped together an impoverished existence on the frontier, many lived in the bustling cities of the eastern seaboard, and some of them rose from humble obscurity to positions of great wealth and power.

Thomas W. Mellon journeyed across the Atlantic in 1818 from Mountjoy in Ulster to Pittsburgh, Pennsylvania, at the age of five. He graduated from the Western University of Pennsylvania, built a distinguished career in law, and established a private banking firm in Pittsburgh. He died one of the wealthiest men in American history.

Mellon's son, Andrew, born in 1855, was a financial wizard in his own right and became an outstanding philanthropist. Andrew left the Western University of Pennsylvania only three months before graduating and started a lumber business. Just as self-sufficient, controlled, and analytical as his father, Andrew also had an uncanny instinct for assessing the worth of new business ideas. The elder Mellon recognized his son's talent and gave complete ownership of the Mellon empire to Andrew, who was only 27 years old at the time.

Andrew Mellon's shrewdness was balanced by his willingness to gamble. He gave financial assistance to the chemist Charles M. Hall—who developed aluminum—and he founded such corporations as the Gulf Oil Company, the New York Shipbuilding Company, and United States Steel. Mellon also backed engineering projects such as the Panama Canal locks, the George Washington Bridge, and construction projects such as the Waldorf-Astoria Hotel. Like many people of Scotch-Irish extraction, Mellon was consumed by his work. At various times, he was director or officer of more than 60 different corporations.

His main business interest, however, remained the family banking legacy. By 1902 Mellon was the president of the banking house formed when the Union Trust Company merged with the T. Mellon and Sons Bank. A failed marriage pushed the taciturn and enigmatic tycoon even further into his work. Finally tired

Andrew Mellon became president of his family's banking firm, served as secretary of the Treasury from 1919 to 1931, and founded several large corporations.

In this dramatic self-portrait, artist Thomas Eakins (1844–1916) gazes intently at the viewer.

of finance, in 1910, Andrew Mellon entered the political arena as a member of the Republican party, which was staunchly probusiness. He resisted the creation of the League of Nations, the forerunner of the United Nations proposed in 1919 by Democratic president Woodrow Wilson, whom Mellon opposed.

When Republican Warren G. Harding came to the White House in 1920, Mellon, who preferred to keep a low profile, reluctantly accepted a cabinet position as secretary of the Treasury. Many objected to his appointment on the ground that Mellon's vast wealth would compromise his policies. From 1919 to 1933, when the Eighteenth Amendment to the Constitution banned the manufacture and sale of liquor, Mellon came under attack for owning the Overholt distillery, even though the operation had long ceased to produce liquor.

Despite this opposition, Mellon scored many triumphs as Treasury secretary, filling the post until 1931. During this time he greatly reduced the national debt and introduced a plan for tax reform criticized for its lenient provisions. In February 1932 Mellon turned from domestic policy-making to diplomacy. He accepted an appointment as ambassador to Great Britain. His foray into diplomacy was short lived, however. As his 80th birthday neared, he returned to the family banking house.

The issue of taxes would come back to plague Andrew Mellon; he became embroiled in a dispute with the federal government over alleged unpaid income taxes. But the evidence against him was not sufficient, and Mellon spent his final years enjoying his leisure and his longtime passion for art. An avid collector since his twenties, Mellon had quietly assembled a private collection worth more than $35 million. In 1937, the year of his death, Mellon founded and funded a parting gift of a great art museum for the nation's capital: the National Gallery.

The diversity of the Scotch-Irish American population led to achievements in many areas. For example, whereas Andrew Mellon used his riches to buy, collect, and bequeath art objects, another Scotch-Irishman, Thomas Eakins (1844–1916), painted some of the most remarkable works produced by an American, including *Max Schmitt in a Scull* and *The Surgical Clinic of Professor Gross*. A later Scotch-Irish painter, Jackson Pollock (1912–1956), invented *action painting*, as the critic Harold Rosenberg called it. This approach to painting stunned the post–World War II art world. Dispensing with brush, palette, and easel, Pollack placed the canvas on the floor, emptied cans of paint onto it, then skillfully directed the flow and shape of the streaming colors. The result was a thick explosion of line and color that pretended to mirror no object other than itself.

President William McKinley took pride in his Scotch-Irish ancestry and praised the group's successful assimilation into American culture.

TOWARD THE FUTURE

The Americanized Scotch-Irishman is the perfection of a type which is the development of the commingling and assimilating process of centuries. Before he loses his racial distinctiveness and individuality he should be photographed by history's camera, although for long years to come his identity will manifest itself in the composite presentment of the future typical American.

—William McKinley, 25th president of the United States (1897–1901)

Three hundred years have passed since the first Scotch-Irish immigrants set foot on American soil. In the interim, the group has undergone considerable change and taken great strides. Linens gave way to buckskins, planting to politics; Bible reading led to newspaper publishing, and the frontier merged with the mainstream.

Today's wildernesses and frontiers are different, more likely to be found in the reaches of space or the cavern of the human mind than on the physical earth. Yet the old-fashioned gumption that made the conquest of continents possible owes much to the high-spirited legacy brought by the immigrants from Ulster in the 18th and 19th centuries. Today, after centuries of intermarriage, vast migration, and general assimilation, few people claim a "pure" Scotch-Irish background.

Nor do many Ulsterians still flock to North America. In the second half of the 19th century, only 28 percent of Ireland's nearly 4 million emigrants—more

Robert Fulton's remarkable new invention, the steamboat, is given a patriotic send-off in 1814.

than 90 percent of whom went to America—came from Ulster. In the 20th century, Scotch-Irish annual emigration plunged from some 55,000 before 1910 to less than half of that before 1914. In 1913 slightly more immigrants from Ulster went to Canada than to the United States. By the 1930s, when the Great Depression wreaked havoc upon economies around the world, Scotch-Irish immigration to America had practically halted.

Yet at the same time that Ulster immigration declined, the Scotch-Irish Americans felt a need to assert their identity, especially in the face of growing immigration from Catholic Ireland. The term *Scotch-Irish*, once a misnomer, became a proud rallying cry. In 1889, the effort to preserve the group's cultural and historical identity led to the founding of the Scotch-Irish Society, which sponsored conventions in Columbia, Tennessee, and Pittsburgh, Pennsylvania. Its members, almost all Presbyterians, included civic leaders such as Robert Bonner, publisher of the *New York Ledger*, and George W. Childs, of the *Philadelphia Public Ledger*. The grandson of American revolutionary and orator Patrick Henry was also a member.

Soon the original Scotch-Irish Society of America inspired the foundation of similar regional organizations, especially in New York State and Pennsylvania.

Many of them responded to developments in the homeland, for example, upholding customary Ulsterian opposition to the Home Rule Act of 1814, which strove to establish a unified and independent Ireland. In 1921, there was almost unanimous rejoicing in the Scotch-Irish community when the Anglo-Irish Treaty succeeded in keeping the six Ulster counties separate from the Republic of Ireland, with their own parliament. One ethnic organization still in existence, Philadelphia's Scotch-Irish Foundation, serves as an official archive of the Ulster Scots' history and accomplishments.

By the mid-20th century, Scotch-Irish Americans had blended so thoroughly into the population that few members of the group attempted to sustain a distinct ethnic identity. Even the intense hostilities between Catholics, who support an independent Northern Ireland, and Protestants, who oppose separaration from British rule, had very little impact on Scotch-Irish Americans. It may be that as European Catholics and Protestants both prospered in North America, serious conflicts between them eventually subsided. An example of this change occurred in 1969, when Ian Paisley, leader of the Protestant Democratic Unionist party (DUP) and the Free Presbyterian church, visited the United States. His denunciation of Catholics in Northern Ireland generated very few favorable reponses from Americans of Scotch-Irish descent.

The pioneer spirit, expressed so intensely in the lives of Sam Houston and Davy Crockett, has perhaps been absorbed into the larger—now more diverse—American character. Because the Scotch-Irish belonged to the first immigrant waves, they played a vigorous role in settling the United States and Canada. When Americans look back at their history's greatest figures, they see a gallery that includes many Scotch-Irish pioneers, soldiers, and statesmen. This ethnic group's dedication to freedom has influenced the lives of subsequent immigrants from around the world, who in turn have gone on to shape their own American frontiers. ✎

FURTHER READING

Anderson, Charles H. *White Protestant Americans: From National Origins to Religious Group*. Englewood Cliffs, NJ: Prentice-Hall, 1970.

Bolton, Charles K. *Scotch-Irish Pioneers in Ulster and America*. Baltimore: Genealog, 1981.

Botkin, B. A., ed. *A Treasury of American Folklore*. New York: Crown, 1944.

Ford, Henry Jones. *The Scotch-Irish in America*. Hamden, CT: Archon Books, 1966.

Glasgow, Maude. *The Scotch-Irish in Northern Ireland and in the American Colonies*. New York: Putnam, 1936.

Graham, James. *Scotch-Irish Canadien Yankee*. New York: Putnam, 1939.

Green, E. R. R., ed. *Essays in Scotch-Irish History*. New York: Humanities Press, 1969.

Green, Samuel S. *The Scotch-Irish in America*. San Francisco: R and E Research Associates, 1970.

Leyburn, James G. *The Scotch-Irish*. Chapel Hill: University of North Carolina Press, 1962.

McCrum, Robert. *The Study of English*. New York: Viking, 1986.

Moore, Arthur. *The Frontier Mind*. Lexington: University of Kentucky Press, 1957.

INDEX

Houston, Robert (grandfather of Sam Houston), 13
Houston, Sam, 13–14, 89, 105

Illinois, 19
impressment, 35
Irish Catholicism, 14, 25, 27, 28, 29, 67, 69, 105

Jackson, Andrew, 19, 69, 86–89, 90, 91, 97
Jackson, Thomas Jonathan ("Stonewall"), 84
James I, king of England, 24, 26
James II, king of England, 31, 32
Jefferson, Thomas, 35, 36, 37, 68, 71
Johnston, Gabriel, 59
Johnston, Robert, 59

Kentucky, 61, 79
Knox, John, 23

Liberal Republican party, 97
Light Horse Cavalry of Philadelphia, 68
Logan, James, 39
Londonderry, New Hampshire, 44, 45, 63
Londonderry, Ulster, 25, 26, 32, 34, 44, 45, 67
Louisiana, 19
Loyal Orange Institution, 69
Luther, Martin, 22

Maine, 42
Makepeace, Francis, 45
Mary I, queen of England, 24
Massachusetts Bay Company, 83
Mather, Cotton, 32
McClellan, George B., 84, 85
McClure, David, 39
McCook, H. C., 17
McCormick, Cyrus, 91

McGuffey, William, 95
McKean, Thomas, 83
McKinley, William, 86, 103
McMillan, John, 58, 59, 81
McNally, Andrew, 95
McNutt, Alexander, 63
Mellon, Andrew, 98–101
Mellon, Thomas W., 98
Methodist church, 65
Mexican War of 1846–48, 85–86
Montgomery, Robert, 84
Moore, Arthur, 79
Morse, Samuel, 91

National Council of Scotland, 27
National Gallery, 101
New Hampshire, 44, 45
New Jersey, 41, 47
New York City, 37, 39, 45, 67
New York State, 19, 41, 45, 46
North Carolina, 41, 59, 86
Nova Scotia, 39, 63
Nullifiers movement, 87

O'Neill, 21
Ozark Mountains, 60

Paisley, Ian, 105
Patrick, Saint, 21
Patterson, Joseph, 58, 59
Paxton boys march, 48
Penn, William, 48
Pennsylvania, 37, 40, 41, 58, 60, 81, 98
Perry, A. L., 73, 80
Perth Amboy, New Jersey, 48
Philadelphia, Pennsylvania, 35, 37, 39, 40, 41, 48, 57, 64, 65, 69
Polk, James K., 85
Pollock, Jackson, 101
Presbyterianism, 15, 18, 23–27, 31–33, 40, 41, 43, 44, 45, 64, 65, 67, 94, 104, 105
Princeton University, 64, 86

Puritanism, 23, 30, 33, 41, 43, 45, 48, 83

Quakers, 48, 57
Quitrents, 48

Reformation, Protestant, 22–23
Reformation, Scottish, 23, 24
Roman Catholicism, 21, 22, 23, 24
Roosevelt, Theodore, 14

San Jacinto, Battle of, 13
Santa Anna, Antonio López de, 13
Scotch-Irish Americans
  areas of settlement in the United States, 40–63
  in Canada, 63, 70
  clothing of, 75–77
  conflict with Irish Catholics, 25, 27, 28, 29, 67, 69, 70, 105
  contributions to American speech, 16
  democracy and, 18, 48, 64, 67, 68, 87
  drinking habits of, 70–72
  emigration from Ireland to the United States, 27, 31, 32–34, 35–37
  emigration from Scotland to Ireland, 24–25
  folk heroes, 61, 89–91
  food staples of, 72–75
  inventors, 91–94
  in Ireland, 22, 25, 26
  journalism and, 19, 45, 94–98
  military leaders, 13, 84, 86
  musical traditions of, 19, 62–63
  origin of the term Scotch-Irish, 14
  as pioneers, 13, 15, 17, 19, 48, 58–63, 64, 71, 74, 75–81, 89–91, 103, 105
  population figures, 18, 19, 103, 104

  reasons for emigration, 27, 31, 32–34, 35
  religious persecution of, 26–27, 30, 31, 32, 34, 41, 43, 44, 46
  reputation as fighters, 79–80
  statesmen, 13, 19, 69, 83–89, 90
  textile trade and, 26, 47, 58
Scotch-Irish Canadian Yankee (Graham), 70
Scotch-Irish Society of America, 104–5
Scotland, 14, 22
Shipton, Clifford, 67
Shute, Samuel, 33, 41
South Carolina, 39, 41, 59, 86, 87
"Star Chamber," 27

Tennessee, 61, 90
Texas, Republic of, 13
Texas, state of, 13
Tithes, 34, 43
"Trail of Tears," 89
Tribune (New York), 97–98

United States Steel, 99
Urban VIII, 28

Virginia, 19, 37, 58, 59, 60

War of 1812, 86
Washington, George, 13, 68, 71
Wentworth, Thomas, 26–27
Whiskey Rebellion, 71
William of Orange, king of England, 32, 69
Wilson, Woodrow, 19, 86, 100
Winthrop, John, 83
Witherspoon, John, 83
Witherspoon, Robert, 59
Wolfe Tone, Theobald, 35
Worcester, Massachusetts, 44, 73

Yamasee War, 59
Yorktown, Battle of, 84

Picture credits

We would like to thank the following sources for providing photographs: The Bettmann Archive: cover, pp. 25, 28, 31, 33, 49, 50, 51, 60, 74, 76, 79, 86, 90, 93, 94, 96, 97, 99, 104; Boatmen's National Bank of St. Louis: p. 72; Bowdoin College Museum of Art: p. 45; British Museum: p. 30; Brooklyn Museum: p. 75; Burndy Library: p. 15; Carnegie Library of Pittsburgh: p. 18; The Fotomas Index: p. 26; The Henry Francis du Pont Winterthur Museum: p. 61; Huntington Library, San Marino, California: pp. 14, 77, 91; Library Company of Philadelphia: p. 68; Library of Congress: pp. 16, 20, 22, 36, 44, 55(bottom right), 56; Courtesy of the Earl and Countess of Malmesbury, Basingstoke, Hampshire, England: p. 85; Mansell Collection: pp. 29, 34; Maryland Historical Society: p. 73; Massachusetts Historical Society: p. 43; Metropolitan Toronto Museum: p. 89; National Academy of Design: p. 100; National Gallery of Scotland: p. 32; National Portrait Gallery: pp. 52, 53, 54, 55(left & top), 58; New York Public Library Picture Collection: pp. 23, 27; Presbyterian Historical Society: pp. 42, 59, 67, 69, 70, 71; San Jacinto Museum: p. 12; States Collection, New York Public Library: pp. 46–47; Washington University Gallery of Art, St. Louis: pp. 38–39; Wisconsin Historical Society: p. 92; Woolaroc Museum, Bartlesville, Oklahoma: p. 88

PETER GUTTMACHER is a free-lance writer living in Brooklyn, New York. He received a B.A. from Connecticut College and an M.A. from New York University.

ROBIN BROWNSTEIN is a free-lance writer living in Brooklyn, New York. She earned a B.A. in journalism from Boston University.

DANIEL PATRICK MOYNIHAN is the senior United States senator from New York. He is also the only person in American history to serve in the cabinets or subcabinets of four successive presidents—Kennedy, Johnson, Nixon, and Ford. Formerly a professor of government at Harvard University, he has written and edited many books, including *Beyond the Melting Pot, Ethnicity: Theory and Experience* (both with Nathan Glazer), *Loyalties,* and *Family and Nation.*